You Want Fries with That?

You Want Fries with That?

A White-Collar Burnout Experiences Life at Minimum Wage

PRIOLEAU ALEXANDER

Arcade Publishing
New York

FIRST EDITION

Library of Congress Cataloging-in-Publication Data
Alexander, Prioleau.
   You want fries with that? : a white-collar burnout experiences life at minimum wage / Prioleau Alexander. —1st ed.
      p. cm.
   ISBN 978-1-55970-864-7 (alk. paper)
   1. Minimum wage—United States. 2. Working poor—United States. 3. Poverty—United States. 4. Alexander, Prioleau. I. Title.
   HD4918.A54 2008
   305.5'62092—dc22
   [B]   2007039961

Published in the United States by Arcade Publishing, Inc., New York
Distributed by Hachette Book Group USA

Visit our Web site at www.arcadepub.com

10 9 8 7 6 5 4 3 2 1

Designed by API

EB

PRINTED IN THE UNITED STATES OF AMERICA

For my friends James Raymond, Mark Russell,
John Tison, and Keith Korman
and my wife, Heidi. Thanks for believing.

If you want to hear God laugh, tell him *your* plans.

Contents

Acknowledgments   *xi*

Prologue: White Collar, Short Leash   1

The Pizza Man Cometh   17

We All Scream, Eventually   48

Why the Roofer Wants to Kick Your Ass   88

Good Things Come in Big Boxes   121

10 ccs of Sanity, Stat . . .   135

You Want Fries with That?   179

Mamas, Don't Let Your Babies Grow Up
    to Be Cowboys   208

Epilogue   *243*

Acknowledgments

Life is a funny thing, and you should never put off until tomorrow what you can do today. So, this seems to be a good time to acknowledge the friendship of the men who've made my life the nonstop adventure it's been: Big T, Tom, John, Gator, Champ, Dove, Capt-Ian, Micky, Mac, Slasher, Iron Mike, Gooner, Doe Eyes, Marine, BD, Pucky, AT, Roomie, Hemi, Elf, Zem, Not-so, Cookie, Drummy, Porter Bill, Striker, Lee, III, Chang, Gunner, Fostah, Dennis, Jay, Frain, Russ, Douglas, Art, The Colonel, BellBoy, BobbyB, Brant, Donny, WorstCase, Captain Sease, Major C, Gern, Labby, Moose, TR, Spreaded, Yang-Ying, McCloud, Yoda, Geoff, DavO, Patch, The Wayne, Jamie, Jimmy, Scooter, Gus, Clark, Robb, Astro, Gerv, Paaarka, Gus, Tombo, Dogg, Rude, Jim, DA, Theo, Todd, Gilly, Stink, Fran, Willie, Robo, Hank, Tummy, Tin Cup, PJ, Dorsey, Davy, Moby, DanO, KC, Christian, Woodrow, JLK, Ken, Eric, Maestro, Johnny, David, Matt, Gaddy, Al, Rick, Chase, Smoak, E, Wolfe, Tim, Dr. PFP, The Marines of the Loose Deuce, Mitch, Chip, Johnny Mac, Tuga, Rrrrick, Hunter, Brennan, Beecher, Ron, Colonel Flag, Charles, Peet, and my nephews Will, Gordon, James, Hayden, Ben, Henry, Joshua, and Mason. I blame each of you for the warped worldview that shouts from the pages of this book.

You Want Fries with That?

Prologue

White Collar, Short Leash

On May 31st of last year, I quit.

Walked away.

Split.

At age forty-one, I leapt from the stern of the foundering SS *Willy Loman* and began my swim against the tide, leaving behind my health insurance, paycheck, and annual bonus.

What inspired this plunge? It's a long and horrific tale, but the blame lies mostly with my chosen profession — the advertising and marketing industry — which is a unique business in a suck-the-life-out-of-you sort of way. In reality, many issues within the profession broke me, so let's skip the excruciating details and cut directly to the chase. The *big* issues were:

1) Advertising is one of the few businesses where clients hire you for your "expertise" and "creativity," only to then begin micromanaging your work to the point of submolecular deconstruction. This gets a bit tiresome

after a decade or so . . . especially when they are taking net 90 to pay their bills.

2) It is also one of the few businesses that produces marked, measurable results, which are somehow invisible to the people who paid for them:

YOU: How'd the new ad campaign do this week?
CLIENT: Okay, I guess. Couldn't really tell.
YOU: Do you want us to keep running it?
CLIENT: No.
YOU: Why not?
CLIENT: For some reason, people came in and bought our entire inventory.

3) And the big one? The advertising game is the only business on the planet where potential clients think they're doing you a *huge* favor by giving you the opportunity to work for them for free. This occurs when, with great pomp and ceremony, a desirable advertising client announces they are undergoing an "agency review," which allows advertising agencies to "pitch" their business. What does this entail? It's too mind-boggling to describe realistically. Instead, let me offer this analogy from the legal profession:

CLIENT WHO NEEDS A LAWYER: Thank you for coming today, gentlemen. I see we have *four* different law firms represented. Excellent. As you might know, I've been charged with trafficking in cocaine, conspiracy to commit murder, and attempted bribery of a federal law enforcement officer. And I'm guilty. So, I've called you all together to offer each of you the chance to work for me. In three weeks, each of you will be allowed to present your detailed ideas for my defense, which you will argue in front of a mock jury of my choosing. I will pick one firm to represent me, and that firm will get paid for the work they've already done. The rest of you will be paid nothing . . . but you can take pride in knowing you had a reputation good enough to be invited to this pitch. Are there any questions or comments?

LAWYERS: Just one: if you have a choice, tell your cellmate you want to be the husband.

Another reason for skirting the excruciating details of my life in the ad game is that you've likely been there too. You know the drill: no matter what your job, if you make good money then it's virtually guaranteed you're swallowing grenades for clients or bosses who don't appreciate your efforts. You endure the madness for the opportunity to make more money, because more money buys more stuff.

Yes, yes, we all know there are some people who love their jobs . . . but only the really lucky folks grow to love Big Brother and connect with his communiqué that SLAVERY IS FREEDOM and WAR IS PEACE . . . As for the rest of us, we trade our time for the necessities, luxuries, and conveniences that money buys. The *new* me, dog-paddling away from my sinking ship of security, figured a person could just eliminate the luxuries and conveniences and get by on the necessities with barely any income at all. After all, our forefathers settled the American West without new clothes or fancy dinners every week, so why not adopt a similar attitude and lifestyle? Just stop spending so damn much money, learn to appreciate the simple things in life, and be like that dude on *Kung Fu*.

My friends failed to understand the brilliance of The Plan.

That was their problem, of course. They didn't get it. They didn't understand the Zen of it all. Mine would be the life of Jimmy Buffett, where margaritas flow from the garden hose, and the soul feeds at leisure on a healthy diet of sunsets, steel drums, and pithy anecdotes of the simple life. A new life was beginning . . . a life of adventure, and discovery. It would be a life in the unknown.

Unfortunately, it takes only a couple of months of "life in the unknown" before several things became very well known:

1) No matter how much you hunker down financially, there are still a few bills that have to be paid, pesky little nonnegotiable items like home insurance, car insurance, life insurance, flood insurance, personal articles insurance, catastrophic health insurance, prescriptions, property taxes, car repairs, home repairs, water bill, electric bill, phone bill, DSL connection, cell phone bill, pest control, in particular termite control, vet bills, and IRA/HSA savings. Friend, that stuff logjams quickly when you don't have a paycheck . . . and if you'll look at the list, you'll notice there isn't a dime budgeted for suntan lotion and margarita mix. Those are bills you have to pay just for the right to suck air here in the land of the free, which, by the way, ain't.

2) When you get married, and the priest announces you are to love and cherish each other for better or worse, richer or poorer, there are exceptions: If, for instance, you quit your white-collar job and six months later you're bitching at your wife because she could have saved fifty cents by buying the ramen noodles by the hundred-pack, and

she tells you to get a job, and you tell her you're still healing . . . well, the priest wasn't including that in the love and cherish part he described during the service. In this particular case, it's completely understandable if your wife chooses to stop cherishing you for a bit.

3) Men and women have different definitions of necessities. Men have a short list: beer. Women have a longer list, which includes things like groceries, haircuts, date nights, cleaning bills, and charitable giving. Women also do not buy the argument that beer is groceries and that if you drink enough of it you won't notice that the cupboard is bare, your hair is a mess, and your clothes look like hell. In addition, drinking beer is a date night in and of itself, and giving one to the wino outside the 7-Eleven on the way to the car is charitable giving. Yes, men and women differ on necessities . . . and women always win the argument, because it's tough to argue with someone who won't speak to you.

4) If you quit your white-collar job, you have plenty of time to ponder life's big questions, the biggest of which is, of course, "How am I going to pay for all this stuff?" You'd be amazed how little you care about what Aristotle has to say about life when you've got the guy from Visa on the phone trying to explain his more existential philosophy on missed credit card payments.

5) If you are not working and your wife is, there is a real discrepancy between her view of a productive day and yours. For instance, if she returns after a hump-busting ten-hour grind and asks what you did with your day, answering, "I shaved," is not sufficient. Nor, apparently, is it funny.

So, there I stood, a man without a job, wondering what to do. By itself, the lack of a job was no big deal, because any potential embarrassment I felt was over-whelmed by internal giddiness about my new freedom — freedom from the *Dilbert* cartoon life that had consumed most of my previous fourteen years. I was just happy to have time on my hands and thus the opportunity to do the items on the Honey-do list my wife would leave every day when she — Okay, that's a lie. The Honey-do list broke me. Within a month, *anything* (except my old job) was preferable to the Honey-do list.

You see, here too, women's minds are very different from men's. While we men turn our brains off for extended periods of time, a woman's mind is always working . . . and if a woman's husband is sitting around during the day and counts shaving on his list of accomplishments, the woman can simply use the man's hands to do the things she'd do if she had the time.

Here's a brief list of the projects the average woman would like done:

a) Tear down the home.

b) Rebuild it much, much better.

c) Take out the garbage.

d) Walk the dogs.

If there was ever a buzz killer in the pursuit of happiness, it would have to be (a), (b), (c), and (d). It's a fact that the reason men object to war less than women — even though it's mostly the men dying — is that during war stuff gets blown up and you don't have to fix it until *after* the war. Ten dollars, which is a lot to me, says that there were *thousands* of men in London sitting in their rockers smiling ear to ear as the bombs rained down during the Battle of Britain.

> WIFE: Worthington! Take cover, for God's sake! A bloody bomb just landed on the garage!
> HUSBAND: No worries, love. I brought the whiskey in from the garage last night.

My plan for dodging the Honey-do list solidified in my mind one evening at a fund-raiser my wife volunteered to assist with. It was the usual cocktail coat-and-tie affair, and my bride sweated away in the kitchen, doing all the work while the nine other folks on the committee supervised her. My mode of operation at a function like this usually entailed finding a friend from the old days, retreating to a corner, and recycling stories about life before side-impact air bags. On this night, however, I found myself cornered by a guy about my age who would not shut up about his legal pro bono work for the foundation whose booze we were drinking. Yes, he'd recently moved to town, and he was making conversation as best he could and was probably nervous about chatting up some local guy he didn't know, but the conversation was agonizing. When he worked into his monologue the details of a "really sweet slip-and-fall case" he'd recently won, I zoned out for fear of voicing my opinion of TV lawyers and getting arrested for hate speech. Then five words came piercing through my defensive web of audio fog.

"So what do you do?"

"Pizza delivery guy," I stated proudly.

Insert sound of crickets.

How does one respond to that? Here is this stuffed-shirt legal scrivener telling me how great he is, and he asks me about my profession. Man, this was a conversation I'd been through a zillion times back in my white-collar life and knew the outcome of without waiting for it to unfold: back then I'd tell him I worked as the creative director of an ad agency, and he'd take control of the conversation again and tell me about his knowledge of advertising and subtly share his opinion that if he just had enough time in the day he could do both my job and his.

But what the hell does he do now?

He's talking with a Pizza Guy, for crying out loud.

What can he ask? If it's fulfilling? If it's challenging? If it's interesting? What is the poor guy supposed to do? As one who has always liked nonconformists, my solution would be to say, "Righteous! Tell me about life as a Pizza Guy." But my new lawyer buddy? He melted down. He said perhaps the worst thing he could have: "No, really . . . what do you do?"

He'd managed to insult me, and I'd never even delivered a pizza. Time to insert the wooden stake in his heart and break it off.

"Really."

Faced with the possibility that he was talking with someone who might not appreciate his sharp intellect and pithy insights, my new pal ended the conversation as quickly as possible and worked his way over to the bar.

Free of Perry Mason, I thought about my comment and wondered about life as a Pizza Guy. What's it like? Who are these guys who arrive at our door bearing the pizza pies we order over the phone? Between you and me, we've probably never met a single human being over the age of twenty-one who delivers pizzas, and yet there are tens of thousands of them around the nation. What's their story? What does the job entail? What's the training like? What happens between the time you call the number to order your thin crust Supremo and the time your doorbell goes ding-dong? There was a multibillion-dollar industry out there cloaked in complete mystery.

Then it occurred to me there were lots of other equally mysterious regular-guy jobs: How about being an Ice Cream Scooper Guy? Or a fast-food employee? Or a construction worker? Or a MegaMart associate? Or a golf caddy?

These are all crap jobs no one wants, but tens of thousands of people have to do them. If they didn't, hell . . . the American economy would collapse. You could lay off half the white-collar people in the United States and nothing bad would happen; in fact, productivity would probably skyrocket! Imagine, if you will, the banishment of every personal injury lawyer, every pollster, every person in advertising and public relations, every sports and entertainment agent, every real estate developer (and nine out of ten Realtors), every local newscasting team, every government bureaucrat, every HMO administrator, and every person with a business card that even hints of middle management. What do *you* think would happen?

And you're right . . . jack-nothing would happen.

Now, imagine an America where the fast-food employees walk off the job for a week. The nation would look like a scene out of *Night of the Living Dead,* with zombies lurching through the streets looking for someone to super-size them. How about the Zippy Marts? Close those for a day, and who would feed the construction workers their morning hot dogs and Mountain Dews? Who would provide the nation's delivery drivers their coffee and Ding Dongs? Where would we the people get our gas, the newspaper, our Lotto tickets, our Cheese Puffs, our beer, and our $6 bean dip? It would be anarchy . . . complete and utter mayhem.

I knew then it was my calling to undertake those jobs. It was time to immerse myself in the madness and experience the ups and downs of life at the bottom. This white-collar burnout would become a person who actually busted his butt for a living instead of someone who talked on the phone and sat in meetings and claimed he busted his butt for a living. I would live those lives and tell those tales.

This is my story.

Responsibility and Intellect Disclaimer

Prior to beginning the story, it's important for you to know that I do understand how unreasonable and irresponsible it was to quit my profession just because it wasn't any fun.

Chances are that you too think, "This sucks," many mornings as you head back into the fray. Please know that I considered what I thought to be the ramifications prior to the actual leap and many times asked myself the question, "Why all the unhappiness?" The answer surfaced as this: it's because — in terms of the human experience — us white-collar Americans have it too easy. We as a nation have come so far, so fast, that our brains cannot adjust. We haven't gotten our mental arms around it. We're surrounded by decadent luxury, while most of the world is trying to figure out how they are going to avoid dying within the week.

To put American white-collar discontent in proper perspective, let's conduct a few interviews with folks around the world who wish they had, well, any kind of collar at all:

YOU: Hey, how's it going?

FATHER OF 4, ETHIOPIA: Well, unless we figure out how to digest sand, I'd say my family has some serious troubles ahead.

YOU: Yeah, but do you feel professionally fulfilled? Are you happy?

FATHER OF 4, ETHIOPIA: I think perhaps we need a translator.

YOU: Excuse me, sir. How's life?

FATHER OF 1, CHINA: My water buffalo died. I am worried I am no longer strong enough to pull the plow myself.

YOU: Man, you really ought to look into a John Deere — all the farmers have 'em. They come in diesel!

FATHER OF 1, CHINA: What is comindeezel?

YOU: Que pasa, mahn?

FATHER OF 3, SOUTH AMERICA: Good news! My children have been offered an extra thirty hours per week overtime at the factory.

YOU: Are they getting options, too?

FATHER OF 3, SOUTH AMERICA: Oh, yes! Of course, working through lunch is still mandatory, but stopping for dinner is now optional.

YOU: I guess you're lovin' life under democracy, huh?

FATHER OF 2, RUSSIA: Oh, yes! Now I keep and sell what I grow.

YOU: Cool. What've you grown?

FATHER OF 2, RUSSIA: Hungry.

If there's one thing that's clear, it's that Americans are light-years ahead of the rest of the world. Our *poorest* people have clothing, way too much food, and — nine times out of ten — shelter with a television. Our middle class lives like the elite of most nations, complete with car, cable, cell phone, fashionable clothing, vacations, and junk food. Our rich . . . well, let's not even bother.

Is there anything wrong with this?

No! Our forefathers made it possible — it is our national damn-did-we-get-lucky birthright. It's just that we, as human beings, aren't ready for it. For tens of thousands of years we've been refining our survival techniques, and suddenly in the past hundred years we've come to consider electricity necessary for survival.

Well, it's not. It's necessary for luxury and sustaining

the lifestyle to which we've become accustomed, but it ain't necessary for survival. Ask the rest of the world.

The fact that we are where we are is the ultimate anomaly, the miracle of miracles, the true testament to the blessings our Creator bestowed on us. We should all be waking up — every day — and staggering out into the sunlight and shouting, "Thank you, God, for allowing *me* to be born in America!"

Do we?

Nope. Instead, we work at our jobs and complain. We do drugs. We drink ourselves silly. We eat so much food we ruin our health. We worship movie stars. We sue tobacco companies and doctors and manufacturers for things that hurt us. We kill each other in droves. And we accept all this as normal.

You know what's normal, in terms of human history? Getting up at sunrise, hunting or farming until sunset, then flopping down in a hut and going to sleep.

Is this good? Does this inspire happiness? Doubtful. But that doesn't make it any less of a fact. The bottom line is that we are immersed in utter lottery-winner luxury, and like most lottery winners we don't know how to handle it.

The saber-toothed tiger is dead; crops magically appear in the grocery store; the mud-and-sticks hovel has been replaced by a cozy little home; fire is conjured at the push of a button; the horse only needs reshoeing every 40,000 miles; our clothing comes from hides that someone else acquired, tanned, and sewed for us; the weather is of no real consequence; and I'll kiss the fanny of any non-Amish American who's mended a pair of socks in the last decade.

In short, all the really hard work is done.

And because we don't really have to take care of ourselves, we no longer take responsibility for ourselves. Everything is beyond our control, it seems. Alcoholism, drug addiction, obesity, gambling, pedophilia — these things are all diseases. If in doubt, we sue. If we choose a life of crime, we blame our parents and society. And if we need an opinion, we look to the television to provide it.

Here is the madness of it: we the people are acting more and more victimized, when in fact we are the least victimized people in the world. In America, it takes exactly one generation to go from an African-American citizen being arrested for riding in the front of the bus to an African-American citizen serving as the chairman of the Joint Chiefs of Staff. It takes zero generations to go from being a computer nerd to the richest man on the planet.

America recognizes talent and tenacity. True, it *is* possible to come up with some groovy invention and not make money, but nine times out of ten that's because the inventor is sitting around the living room waiting for Wall Street to call. If you've got talent *and* tenacity, this nation is your oyster.

Is this possible in any other nation?

No.

Why?

Because they didn't have Thomas Jefferson and a team

of the greatest thinkers in history create their nation from scratch. Their nations were created like, well, Jell-O, where eventually over time things just sort of jelled into place. Then unjelled. Then jelled.

Socialism doesn't work.

Communism doesn't work.

Fascism doesn't work.

Anarchy doesn't work.

Feudalism doesn't work.

The world has been there, tried that . . . and only one system works really well.

Ours.

I understand this, and embrace this. The trials and tribulations associated with dropping out of the rat race to pursue a different and unpredictable path were brought *on* me *by* me. The fickle finger of blame points directly at me, and me alone. It is I who do not fit, and I bear no ill will towards the system that serves the American people so well. Dropping out is not wise, nor is it freeing.

It is, however, pretty funny at times.

The Pizza Man Cometh

For my first bottom-rung position, I decided to live up to the comment made to my attorney-at-law buddy and experience the life of America's most beloved road warrior: the Pizza Delivery Guy. How many times in your life has the Pizza Guy rung the doorbell at your home? Hundreds? And yet most likely you've never had any personal interaction with a single one of them. You love them, you need them, but you've never noticed them. Hell, the average American wouldn't notice if it was the Elephant Man delivering their pizza, even if he took the money with one hand, made change with the other, then handed over the pizza with his trunk. *Hey, here's the check, thanks, bye.* If ever there was a job with minimal client interaction, this had to be it. After my overload of client interaction, it sounded like heaven.

Before taking the plunge, I decided to do a little research on the history of pizza and Googled the topic to see what could be learned. Right away it became clear that most folks give the Greeks the nod for the initial concept of pizza . . . but the initial concept for pizza isn't that complex, is it? Conceptually, aren't we just talking about a sandwich where you forget to finish making the sandwich? And because this sandwich doesn't actually sandwich the ingredients, doesn't this result in all the olives and goat cheese falling into your lap? History may give the Greeks the conceptual credit, but that's really not reason enough to get all historically maudlin. They may have sat on rocks, too, but I don't see them getting any royalties from the La-Z-Boy Recliner Corporation.

Pizza, as *we* know it, was invented by an Italian baker named Raffaele Esposito in Naples, Italy, in 1889. He'd been fooling around with different kinds of dough and baked cheese into it, and came up with a pretty tasty treat, especially if you slathered a little tomato sauce on it. Word got out about his new invention, and King Umberto and Queen Margherita wanted a taste. For the big dinner, Raffaele went completely crazoid and built a pizza that included toppings containing the colors of the Italian flag: white mozzarella cheese, green basil, and red tomato sauce. The king and queen dug in like a couple of blunt-crazed Rastafarians and declared pizza to be a most righteous treat.

Before long pizzerias popped up all over Italy, which proved to be fortunate in the long run: when the American army swept through the nation in World War II, the Italians were able to appease the soldiers with pizza, and who wants to pillage and burn when you're struggling to overcome a food coma induced by a deep-dish pepperoni? When the GIs returned home from the war, they brought with them a serious jones for the stuff.

The rest, of course, is history. Today pizza is a $32 billion-a-year industry. In America alone we mow through over a hundred acres of pizza a day (which, by the way, is about 350 slices of pizza every second). The single biggest hour in the history of American pizza deliveries was when O.J. led police on a low-speed chase through L.A. There are over sixty thousand pizzerias in the U.S., and each year every man, woman, and child in America would have to shovel down over twenty-three pounds of pizza to account for the tons consumed.

And me? All I wanted was a little slice of that multibillion-dollar pie.

The Plunge

The first thing you should know about becoming a Pizza Delivery Guy is that you aren't just hired for it: you *sign up* for it. I'm pretty sure the interview process is stricter for joining that team of radical Muslims who go stomp around in minefields to detonate mines. The process in my case started with me driving to the closest national pizza chain, ferreting out the manager, and simply asking for a job. He looked at me like I'd volunteered to go stomping around in minefields.

"There's a training session at our Waterfield Avenue store every Thursday night at seven p.m.," he said. "Go to that, then come back here."

Interview complete.

Upon my arrival at the Waterfield Ave. store the following Thursday, the counter help directed me back to a small, gray interrogation-type room, where a second employee ordered me to take a seat among the other twelve new recruits. In the five seconds it took for me to scan the crowd, it became clear that exactly two of them appeared trustworthy enough to clean the kudzu out from behind my old office building. The other ten either reeked of car trouble or, well, reeked period. If they'd drug-tested us as a group, Hunter S. Thompson would have returned from the grave just to meet the gang and pay his respects.

After a couple of minutes, a very handsome, tan, and physically fit guy walked in and began our training. He told us that he'd sold his nine franchises in order to move to town and become the operations manager for the local franchisee. "Ah, so," I thought, "he's not only handsome, tan, and fit, he's rich." It occurred to me he might be the matter to our collective antimatter, and that if he touched one of us the universe might explode.

Mr. Tan-'n'-Fit then began to train us, and he did an excellent job. He stood up there in front of a crowd of stone-faced, slack-jawed potential employees and actually took the time to try and make the session interesting and humorous. (No one laughed at his jokes, however, because he didn't use the word "fart" in any of his punch lines.) We learned about company history, general operations, safety, and the fact that they did not discriminate in their hiring, which is the understatement of the century. After an hour they served us some pizza, trained us for another hour, and made us take a written test roughly on par with the quizzes you find on the back of a Cap'n Crunch box. Then they issued our shirts and caps.

Training complete.

In that moment I began to truly understand the genius of these national pizza delivery companies. Think of it — they have an entire financial empire built on the backs of employees so unreliable that employment sessions run year-round, just to replace the latest crop of employees who quit because they made enough money to get their bong out of hock.

Do you realize how far you've got to dumb things down for stoners, nerds, burnouts, knuckleheads, teenagers, and English majors to do them correctly? Can you imagine trying to organize and run a business where this band of misfits takes your orders, makes your product, and delivers said product via face-to-face contact with the client? My Lord, merely thinking about the *potential* problems could cause a management professional to call in dead. But, then again, consider what a testament this is to the nation we live in! How mind-boggling is it that we live in a country where a guy with some motivation and smarts can build this kind of empire from scratch? An entire *continent* of Cold War commies couldn't manufacture one decent car or get their stupid potatoes to grow, but here in America a guy dumbs down the art of pizza delivery and, within one lifetime, he's built a multibillion-dollar empire using only employees stupid enough to — well, stupid enough to quit their white-collar job and become a Pizza Guy.

Anyone who goes through pizza training is bound

to leave the event inspired: the American dream *works* . . . provided you haven't been so crushed by the American dream that you're willing to deliver pizzas for a living.

The Road Warrior

My next step was calling the manager of "my" store, and he told me to be at work the following day at 5:00 p.m. The store was located a mere ten-minute commute from my house, so I left at 4:40. Needless to say, my progress was delayed by a wreck on the en route bridge and the materialization of a new road construction area, so I didn't make it into the store until 5:10. Being a former Marine and a maniac about promptness, I would have fired me on the spot.

"Sorry about this," I told him. "It's unprofessional to show up late, especially since this is my first day."

The manager looked at me curiously. "Who are you?" he said.

"Prioleau. Pray-Lowe. Your new driver."

"Okay, Lowe," he said, "follow me. Let me show you how to clock in." It didn't occur to him to be angry with a driver for being late, any more than it would occur to me to spank my dog for licking his privates.

The manager worked out of . . . well, a closet would be the most accurate description. He leaned over a keyboard, which was hooked up to a computer that was obviously purchased from Houston Mission Control after Apollo

One made it safely home. Impressive. *PC Magazine* reported recently that at least a fifth of our gross national product is a result of unnecessary computer upgrades made by managers trying to get their employees to just shut up about upgrades. The sheer willpower it takes to run a company utilizing only sufficient computing power is nothing less than Herculean, and is almost unheard-of within corporate America's management structure.

"Okay, Lowe," he said, "when you come in, hit F10 to bring up this screen, tab down to E, hit Enter, type in your employee number, hit Enter, wait for this screen to come up, then hit Enter two more times, hit F10 again, scroll down to Dispatch, and hit Enter again. Got it?"

Panic and horror overcame me. *I was too stupid to be a Pizza Delivery Guy.*

"Got it."

"Follow me," he said.

Next stop, the dispatch area — sort of like the ready room on an aircraft carrier, where the pilots await their target briefing. To the left stood the warming racks, where the pizzas sat when they were boxed and ready for delivery. To the right were the mobile oven bags, which cost $140 apiece because they have some sort of cold-fusion chip inside them that gets charged, then radiates the heat necessary to keep the inbound pizza hot. In between these stations lay a keyboard and computer monitor (serial number 000000002 — so old it has to be the second computer ever made).

"You see your name up on the dispatch list?" my boss asked. "When it gets to the top, you'll see an address next to it. That's your run. You punch in your employee number and hit Enter. Then punch in the order number and hit Enter four times. Grab the pizza, and you're outta here."

"Why do I hit Enter four times?"

The attention span the manager set aside for training new employees drained out of his eyes.

"This is Mickey," he said pointing to a clean-cut, all-American guy of about thirty. "He's been driving for four years. He can answer any questions you have."

"Mickey," I said, "I'm Lowe. Why do you hit Enter four times?"

"Lowe," he said, "there are some mysteries that man wasn't meant to solve. Just hit Enter four times."

"Four times. Roger that."

"Now," Mickey said, "here's some of the stuff you'll need to know: When your pizza lands on the warming rack, there's an adhesive ticket on it. Pull it off, and stick it upside down on your pants, just above your right knee. That way, when you're driving, you can look down and read it if you forget the address or need the phone number."

Oh yeah, baby — like a World War II bomber pilot with his target data.

"Before you stick it on your pants, read it carefully. It will tell you how many pizzas there are in that order, and it has a spot here where it says *other*. If there's a zero by *other*, it's just a pizza run. If there's a *number* by *other*, it means they've ordered something else as well. The number tells you how many *other* things there are. To find out what, you look over on the actual pizza box, and it will say, you know, like a Coke, or some dessert, or some wings."

"Got it," I said, completely confused. Sure, it sounds easy to you, you nabob, sitting on your butt reading this . . . *but baby,* I was in the belly of the beast! The phones rang, the flour flew, and the drivers jockeyed for the pole position. A mortal like you might have panicked, but rest assured "the Kid" was strappin' on his game face.

"Okay," said Mickey, "see your name at the top? There's the address . . . 1011 Lake Hunter Circle. Punch in your employee number. Hit Enter. Punch in the order number right there. Hit Enter four times. Okay, you're outta here."

The Kid made his move. He panicked.

"You mean I'm supposed to deliver that pizza?"

"Exactly."

"Where the hell is 1011 Lake Hunter Circle?"

"There's a big detailed map of the area in the back," Mickey said. "But I can tell you. Take Leeds over to Mathis, turn right, and your fourth subdivision will be Westlake. Turn in there, go three streets, and take a left on Shetland Court. The second right is Lake Hunter, and uh, the odd numbers are on the left. I'm thinking 1011 will be about ten houses down."

"Surely you're kidding, right?"

"No," he said, "and don't call me Shirley."

The oldest joke in the book, and my brain couldn't absorb it for the overload of all the mission-critical data.

"Go, man. Time's burning."

"Aren't I supposed to ride with someone tonight?" I asked.

"Dude, you're delivering pizzas," Mickey said. "There's no residency required."

Four minutes after clocking in, and my first pizza was outbound.

Trade Secrets Unveiled

There are, of course, plenty of things you're dying to know about this most noble trade, and *some* can be shared. Some cannot, of course, due to my loyalty to the company, and my fear of their long arm. To admit the actual number of pepperonis on a large hand-tossed would be as heinous as spilling the beans on Ingredient X in Coca-Cola, or smuggling out a sample of the Big Mac special sauce for analysis.

Anyway, here are some answers to some frequently asked questions:

First, how many pizzas do you take out with you on a run?

That's an easy one, because corporate policy sums up the answer in a brilliantly devised ditty: *One* pizza . . . best way. *Two* pizzas . . . okay. *Three* pizzas . . . no way!

Do the drivers all adhere to this policy? For an answer one must refer to the movie *Top Gun* and the very realistic cast of characters it featured. The yin and yang of the movie were Maverick and Iceman: Maverick known for his daring "seat-of-the-pants flying" (accented by limitless skill and wisecracks to his NFO Goose) and Iceman known for his extremely disciplined by-the-book tactics and his ability to "wear an opponent down" (with no wisecracking whatsoever). Given that Pizza Guys are virtual clones of F-14 pilots, it goes without saying that similar personalities emerge.

A new driver, of course, delivers like the Iceman, looking to corporate policy to guide his tactics and strategies. This is because new drivers are still a little nervous about the whole process and think it matters that the pizza arrives fresh and hot. New drivers are also fools and make very little money.

Eventually, drivers come to understand that the real secret is in volume. This is because you are tipped (and gone) by the time the customer opens his pizza and discovers it's become a frozen-dough Frisbee. At my store there was this one guy, Dirk Steele, who scoffed at the company policy and would regularly grab three pies for a run. And as irritating as his cavalier attitude towards the "best way" might have been, that guy could deliver the goods. He worked like a wizard on the keyboard, dispatching himself multiple pizzas, double-packing the mobile oven bags, orchestrating routes with multiple traffic escape avenues and Double Rs (rights on red), and chewing up blacktop with his delivery bubble turned off. Dirk was . . . was . . . okay, he's a figment of my imagination. But let there be no doubt that there are Dirk-type characters out there right now, delivering by the seat of their pants and dazzling their female customers with their icy good looks and Ray-Ban Aviator sunglasses. Just because he didn't work at my store doesn't mean he didn't exist.

*   *   *

The next question friends frequently asked was, "Did you help make pizzas?"

The answer is "No."

Why? Because a national pizza company is a machine, and that machine has two primary functions: sell pizza, and get people off the clock as fast as possible.

As a result, the drivers are scheduled to walk in the door the moment the orders start piling up. You walk in, wash your hands, and start dispatching yourself pizzas. When you return from that run, there are pizzas on the warming rack already falling behind the time curve. You dispatch and go; dispatch and go; dispatch and go. This time of the day — when everyone was in a rush — was creatively referred to as *the Rush*. Sunday through Thursday, the Rush phone calls start at 5:50 p.m. and end abruptly at 8:10. (The Friday and Saturday Rush runs until 8:35.) Now, since it takes exactly ten minutes to field a call, take the order, make the pizza, run it through the oven, box it, and cut it, that means deliveries during the Rush start going out the door at exactly 6:00 p.m. So guess what time most of the drivers clocked in? Then, at some time after 8:20, you'd return to see no pizzas on the warming rack, and the first thing you'd hear as you entered the store was one of the managers say, "All right . . . let's get you clocked out."

All of us employees, of course, yearned to loiter around and play grab-ass on the clock, but the *machine* doesn't allow for such monkeyshines. When you're on the clock, you're working . . . When you're *not* working, you're off the clock.

I distinctly remember my fourth night, when the only words I said inside the store to my fellow employees were "Thanks, boss," as he tallied my bank and gave me my tips.

This pace and workflow system is awesome for making the corporation money, but not so awesome if you're trying to get to know your fellow employees. The drivers are always in a rush to get the next pizza out the door and simply don't have time to exchange thoughts on issues like an upcoming Supreme Court nominee. To drivers, other drivers are just delivery drones (who might deprive them of a "good tip" run). No one ever copped much of an attitude, and the drivers where I worked seemed to be really nice guys, but . . . well, Maverick and Iceman never buddied around together, and neither did we.

Another frequent question is "What kind of money did you make?"

That's an easy answer: not much. You make minimum wage on the clock, plus tips, which you must declare to the government. At the end of the night you've made about $30 in tips for three hours' work. This feels great, right up to when you put $20 in gas in your car on the way home. For a Pizza Guy, one must also remember that work comes in three- to four-hour increments. To go from making pocket change to making a living, you had to move into the Management Slavery Program, which requires a two-pack-a-day cigarette habit and a willingness to manage people like, well, me.

The inside guys, who make the pizzas and answer the phones and clean the place, make a higher hourly wage, but how much more is a mystery. I tried to find out once, but the conversation went like this:

> ME: Hey, Scott . . . How much do you inside guys make per —
> MANAGER: Lowe! Aren't you off the clock?
> ME: Yeah, I'm headed out. I just wanted —
> MANAGER: Lowe! If you're *off* the clock, you *aren't* insured. If you fall and bust your coconut, we got no liability coverage. Now, git!
> ME: Yes, boss.

And with that, the machine ejected me out the door into the civilian world.

During my time as a Pizza Delivery Guy, the most frequent question I received from friends was "How much should I tip the Pizza Guy?"

Good question. And my standard response was, "How much do you tip a waitress? At the most, the waitress has to take a few steps and refill your iced tea . . . and invests maybe five actual minutes in the servicing of your specific needs."

Now, let's consider the Pizza Pie Road Warrior: This guy is given work in three- to four-hour chunks, but he's willing to give up all his evening plans in order to make some much-needed cash. He gets in a vehicle — which he maintains and insures at his own expense — and drives across town to deliver your meal to your front door. He finds your address in the dark, parks, and all but puts dinner on your kitchen table.

And you tip him, what? Two or three bucks?

How much did you tip your waitress at the last fancy dinner you ate? After a nice meal with a few other couples, it's not uncommon for a waitress to scoot with a cool $100 . . . without so much as a run to her car for the salt and pepper. She takes your order, brings your beer (which is admittedly no small task with me and my friends), and puts your food down in front of you.

Hmmm . . . sounds familiar: Take order, *check*. Get dinner, *check*. Deliver to person doing the eating, *check*.

Now, let's say you got sick and missed this fancy meal with your friends . . . but your friends ordered for you any-way, and a waitress going off duty drove across town to deliver the meal to your home. Not only would you need a grocery bag for her tip, you'd be falling all over yourself gushing about how wonderful she was.

I know, I know . . . before being a Pizza Guy I'd have come up with the same responses: *Well, it's the Pizza Guy's job. I didn't ask him to work there. He knows what he's in for. It's not my fault he needs to work for extra cash. He should have done what I did, and properly planned when choosing his parents.*

But here's the depressing news about me and you, Mr. and Mrs. Gated-Community-Million-Dollar-Home . . . We tip less than migrant workers who kill themselves for $6 an hour. We tip less than people with missing front teeth. We tip less than people who live in trailer parks. You and I are like the grandmother who offers the teenage grandson "a whole quarter" to rake the yard. But that ain't me anymore. They'll plant me in the ground before I ever again tip a

Pizza Guy less than five bucks. You may use that as your tip guide if you choose.

Before closing this section, let me explain why you never get much of a song and dance from your driver. You see, I figured I'd make a killing delivering pizzas, simply by going out of my way to be nice, and funny, and presentable. Sadly, it never made me much extra money, because ninety percent of the folks who order pizzas write a check *with the tip included* five seconds after they hang up the phone. With the check already written, a driver could be juggling chainsaws with bananas stuffed up his nose and the pizzas balanced on his head and he ain't getting a revised (and bigger) tip. After several months of peppy interaction, most drivers just give up on being cute and focus on praying that you didn't stiff them for two bucks or less.

Sometimes the Bear Gets You

There is an old expression that says, "Sometimes you get the bear, and sometimes the bear gets you." One Tuesday night, our entire team watched in horror as the bear got my boss.

Remember, at these national pizza stores, it's all about labor costs. The machine is designed to get you off the clock as quickly as possible. However, the machine has a problem, in that humans run it . . . and humans sometimes fail to respect the power of the bear.

So, here's what happened on Black Tuesday. We all arrived for the Rush at the appointed, uh, minute, and the

Rush didn't materialize. One by one we arrived, and at 6:05 p.m. the dispatch area overflowed with drivers and inside workers standing around looking at each other. This, of course, is strange and uncomfortable, because you can work at a pizza delivery place for a year and not know anyone's name, so what do you chat about? (*Yeah, I'm here because I bought a double-inverted, humpback Growler from Honest Sammy's Used Cars at twenty-seven percent interest then totaled it before the insurance kicked in. How 'bout you?*) My boss, of course, was in a total freakin' meltdown at the idea of all these minimum-wage workers running up a tab on the corporate account, but he knew the Rush might start.

Tick-tock, tick-tock. What to do, what to do?

At 6:15, he decided that this would be a slow night. He sent home all his insiders and two drivers. At 6:17, the phone system exploded like a Web site posting just-discovered nude photos of Jessica Simpson. The bear was in the tent with us.

Now, not having worked at a pizza place, you're probably wondering why this is a big deal. Let me explain: because the drivers clock in and out with such exact precision, they receive almost zero cross-training in things like entering orders from the phone, making and labeling boxes so the right pizza goes in the right box, or even making the pizzas. On Black Tuesday, I knew how to do exactly none of these things.

At 6:17 when the Rush began, my boss happened to be the only guy in the store who knew how to take orders, label boxes, and make pizzas. And for the next thirty minutes, he did nothing but put people on hold and take orders. Unfortunately, this meant that every single pizza would be late before it was made. This is not good, especially since the computer records all in and out times and factors them into the store's monthly averages, which factors into my boss's bonus, which factors into his mood.

Out of sheer panic a couple of the veteran drivers jumped in and made pizzas, but this hardly put a dent in the logjam. In fact, their efforts proved self-defeating, because once the pizzas they made came out they had to be delivered, which prevented them from making more pizzas, because they had to deliver the pizzas they'd made.

As an added torture nugget, Black Tuesday also turned out to be a big night for folks walking into the store to order carryout. This forced the boss man to ignore the forty-two people currently on hold, take the face-to-face carryout orders at the counter, and make *those* pizzas while the customers stood there.

I chose Black Tuesday as a night to get lost on a delivery, and my customer chose Black Tuesday to give a phone number that was disconnected. That, my friend, is a helpless feeling: no way to call back to the store, because boss man wouldn't be able to stop and check the map for me, and my customer lived in a part of town where you don't just stop to chat about directions with the nearest felon.

Eventually, random turning put me in front of the right trailer, and the guy received his pizza. Thanks to the cold-fusion mobile oven (and the fact that it was about one degree outside), the pizza steamed when it emerged, which made the guy happy. I got back to the store and logged myself back in, at which point the computer screen congratulated me for shattering the record for the worst delivery time in the store's history. My attempts to figure out how to assign the run to another driver went poorly, chiefly because my operator skill set was limited to hitting Enter a lot.

My boss was now able to make pizzas in frenzied spurts, and he would throw them onto the oven conveyer belt and never give them another thought. This tactic resulted in a festive little pizza parade marching through the oven, all of them bound for a collision course with the floor at the end of the very short conveyer-belt-guided parade route. I entered the store moments before the lead pizzas dropped off the edge and — springing into what passed for action — began taking them off the conveyer to box and cut them. I had no clue which pizza went into which box (due to a lack of training in the coding system), but, hey, the customers were going to get something round and flat, and that would have to be good enough.

Of course, the longer my new job as boxer/cutter lasted, the later the first-out pizzas got . . . but the boss still had forty-two people on hold and two walk-in customers clamoring for his attention, so there was little that could be done about it. I continued to put round, flat things in boxes until another driver got back, at which time a hopelessly late delivery demanded my exit from the premises. It is a mathematical certainty that at least half the pizzas were loaded into the wrong boxes, but if anyone called in on Black Tuesday to complain about getting the wrong pizza, I never heard about it . . . probably because when they called they got put on hold so long that they just gave up and ate the peanut butter and bacon pizza they got.

At 9:50, the Rush was over. Boss man looked no worse for the wear, which impressed me: I thought of us Marines as the only people trained to do the impossible with nothing, yet he'd handled the madness nicely — and without the benefit of knowing he might get to shoot someone as a reward. Surely the ol' boss man would want to chat a while and talk about our pulling together and the subsequent survival of the bear attack. It would be a chance for us to do some shared-suffering-type bonding and build up some serious esprit de pizza.

"Lowe," he said, "get your stuff and let's get you clocked out."

Corporate Publications

In the very rare moments available for standing around on slower nights, I made a point of wandering around and reading whatever corporate stuff I could. The sight of the publications and posters always made me chuckle, because I could envision how many zillions of dollars the Mother Ship spent developing the material, and how many hundreds of revisions it went through as every yo-yo at HQ put in their two cents.

> CREATIVE DIRECTOR: . . . and the poster will say, "Perfect crust is a must!"

BRAND MANAGER: Hmmm . . . is "perfect" a strong enough word?

ASSISTANT VP OF SALES: How about "extraordinary"?

ART DIRECTOR: Or "flawless"?

VP OF MARKETING: I think "delicious" is the right word. It has a *food* feel to it.

ASSISTANT VP OF MARKETING: Another great idea, boss!

OPERATIONS MANAGER: Will our people on the front lines embrace it?

VP OF FINANCE: Do extra letters cost more?

ASSISTANT TO CEO: The Big Guy wants results from this poster . . .

BRAND MANAGER: Okay, let's put together focus groups in Chicago, New York, Atlanta, Dallas, San Diego, and Des Moines. Everyone clear their calendars next week — this is hot, and we all need to be there. Everyone in?

CREATIVE DIRECTOR: Darn, can't make it. I've decided to kill myself tonight.

When each project was done, I'm sure everyone felt proud, from the CEO on down. Quite frankly, it's easy to understand the Puzzle Palace's attraction to this stuff, given that the actual creativity and ingenuity vanished from the company five years after the founder started the business. From there, it's just been repetition with really expensive publications and posters.

One day I snuck onto the clock ten minutes early and thus had ten minutes to do nothing. I found the *Driver's Standard Operating Procedures Manual* under a box of napkins behind the pineapple cans, and gave it a read. There were a number of SOPs that indicated the Mother

Ship folks needed to spend a little more time down in the trenches. Here are a few examples:

Accepting Checks: The manual takes about a page to unfold these nuggets of wisdom and explains that accepting a check requires visual verification of the customer's driver's license, the current address printed on the check, a phone number, a driver's license number, a second form of identification, and, hell, get a DNA sample while you're at it. In reality, drivers would do well to adhere to one requirement above all: when accepting a check, make sure it is actually made out to our company. This would have proved helpful to, say, me, because one night I accepted a check from some stoner idiot that I later discovered to be made out to our biggest competitor. At the end of my shift, I reluctantly drove out to get a correct check (off the clock). For my trouble, the guy wrote me another check for the same amount, with nothing for the extra effort. (In retrospect, perhaps *he* wasn't the idiot.)

Dealing with Customers at the Door: This is half a page of nonsense and includes tips about your greeting, how to answer questions, and how to generate an overall atmosphere of hustle. (It all but says, "Fake like you're breathing hard.")

In reality, a corporate team with a clue would offer such actually useful hints as:

1) Stand downwind if you burn a doobie en route.

2) Avoid screaming at the customer as to why he both-

ers to give a freakin' street number if he is too freakin' stupid to have a freakin' number on the freakin' house or mailbox.

3) After receiving a one-dollar tip, avoid the words, "Gee, mister! A whole dollar! Keen! I can buy myself some marbles now!"

What to Do at a Suspicious Address: This little gem went on for two pages, with more safety precautions than a kindergarten's bazooka-shooting class. "*We are so concerned for our **drivers' safety** that we are willing to talk about **drivers' safety** in a real company publication, and to prove it we will use the word **safety** dozens of times and sometimes put **safety** in **bold italics**.*" All very nice and safe, but among us drivers down on the street, the rule of thumb is: establish covering fire if necessary, but get the pizza to the door and get that money.

In Case of Robbery: Like the whole "suspicious address" diatribe, this read simply as anti-lawsuit drivel: Don't resist . . . Cooperate . . . Give them the money and the pizza . . . blah, blah, blah. Hey, in case no one has noticed, pizza drivers need money so bad they're willing to deliver pizzas for it. If you want to give me *useful* advice about a robbery situation, your guidance needs to be more along the lines of: "When firing at a robber, resist the urge to take a head shot — aim for the center of his chest."

Cooperate? Right. Just tell us if your research shows

that a 9mm can do the job, or if I need to upgrade to a .40 caliber.

A couple of weeks later, I found a different set of SOPs — this one for the customer service reps. CSRs are the guys who answer the phones and make the pizzas. These SOPs were similarly written by a group of people who'd never actually *been* in a pizza delivery place and possibly never actually met one of these mysterious CSRs. Among the gems of wisdom they provide to the insiders are:

Communicating with the Drivers: What the Puzzle Palace wants from the insiders in this regard is essentially adult supervision. They urge the insiders to "remind the Drivers to buckle up" and "watch for unsafe driving practices as the Drivers leave and return." Very good, theoretically. However, since 99.8 percent of an insider's time is spent facedown in a computer screen taking orders or facedown over the prep counter making pizzas, the actual wording should have been a little different — perhaps something like, "Although you may never see them, the company employs people known as Drivers. If you see someone you don't know behind the counter, don't panic and give him all the money in the till: chances are good he is a Driver."

Suspicious People in the Store: This is an extended version of the driver's robbery advice but gives tips about how to make the "suspicious person" feel less like robbing the store. Many of the ideas are good ones but are encumbered by two main problems: First, it's hard to be suspicious when you're either taking orders, making pizzas, or in the process of clocking out. Second, the money in the store belongs to some stinkin'-rich franchisee, so who's going to bother?

This section needs to be much shorter and should say simply, "When clocking out, be sure to tell the manager if a robbery occurred during your shift."

Dealing with Customers in No-Delivery Zones: This entire section is priceless, and as a public relations/media relations veteran, I can assure you it was written by an attorney/public relations team. Why? Because No-Delivery Zones are a discrimination lawsuit waiting to happen. As a result, the section is written in a "If *they* say . . . then *you* say" style.

One can only assume the folks at the Puzzle Palace aren't aware that the average insider is an eighteen-year-old high school senior and will sound a little funny saying, "I share your frustration, but our first priority is the safety of our Drivers. Our management team is monitoring the situation closely, and we'll be happy to notify you if circumstances change. I'll be happy to take down your number. [*Note: You gotta love the next sentence.*] We do offer carryout . . . would you like to pick your pizza up? We can have it ready in fifteen minutes."

Now, let's be real. How is the average teenage male going to handle this? Let's listen in, shall we? "Sorry, we don't deliver there. Why? 'Cause it's a war zone, that's why! You know how much crime has to be reported for us not to go there? We deliver in freakin' Baghdad, dude. Hey, chill, bud . . . I'm just sayin' nobody's willing to die for a two-dollar tip. You're gonna sue me? Big frickin' deal. Well, kiss my donkey-donk butt, too, ya crack-neighborhood-livin' freak!"

Driven to the Brink

If there is one aspect of the job that tortures a driver like flaming bamboo shoots shoved under his fingernails, it is this: *the absence of numbers on houses.*

Now, seriously, let me ask you: if a friend is coming over to your house for the first time, would you give him or her a numbered address if you had no numbers on your house or on your mailbox? I suppose if you're stupid enough not to have numbers on your house or mailbox you *might,* but . . . come on, people! How are the cops supposed to find you? The repairman? The cable guy? The pizza guy? Ed McMahon? The frequency of houses with no numbers was so great that over a two-shift period I experimented by asking customers, "Is there a number out here that I just didn't see?"

The standard response? "Uhh, no."

The response they should have given? "No, there's not. And that's a good question. How did you find me? You must be a genius. Here's a twenty-dollar bill for not giving up."

The single worst address was 1066 Johnnie Dodds Blvd. Johnnie Dodds is a retail frontage road, so the law of averages insisted it was a store (which would no doubt have street numbers affixed to the front). I called the phone number and got an answering machine. My second call a few minutes later again connected with a machine. The pizza was boxed and cut, so I grabbed it and left, assuming a solution to the problem would emerge in the car. The stores along Johnnie Dodds refused to yield a number 1066. The only thing left was the entrance to Crickentree, an apartment complex with twenty-four buildings and eight apartments per building. *No one* — no human on the entire planet — is so stupid he'd give an apartment complex as his address.

I dialed the number on my cell phone. Again, the machine.

"This is Lowe," I said into the machine, "the Pizza Guy. I can't find your address, and you're not answering the phone, so I'm going to have to — "

"Hello?" a voice croaked.

"This is Lowe. I've got your pizza. Where is 1066?"

"Crickentree."

I was incredulous. "Okay, *where* in Crickentree?"

"Umm, come to the stop sign, and turn right, and then take your second left, and come down, and you'll see some people in front of my building."

"Terrific, but maybe you could give me a landmark that won't walk away."

"Umm, there's a tarped car out there."

"Of course there is," I thought.

Finally, we connected. The guy could not have been more stoned if you removed his brain and soaked it in a bowl of bong water. As the pizza changed hands, I asked, "How did you think I was going to find you?"

"Y'all have delivered here before. And I figured if you got lost, you'd call."

"I did. You were screening your calls."

"Oh, yeah," the guy said. And left with his pizza.

It was my last run of that night. I went home to drink beer and wonder if that guy canceled out my vote in any elections.

Under the Bubble

When you're out on the road driving alone with that big neon pizza bubble atop your car, you have plenty of time to think. And since your job is delivering pizzas, you don't have that much to think about. So it's, well, a good time to think.

Among the things that occurred to me was that the bubble is less of an advertisement, and more of a huge sign that announces "I dare you" to drivers in every direction. This revelation occurred after a few days, as it became clear that everyone would simply get the hell out of my way, especially in the kind of tricky judgment situations that often result in bent fenders, hurt feelings, and happy TV lawyers. I pondered the issue and tried to consider all the angles, and then it finally dawned on me: people think Pizza Guys still operate under the thirty-minutes-or-it's-free rule and thus are willing to die to make that bootleg turn through oncoming traffic. The bubble says to the average Joe, "Driver willing to die for the right of way." As a result, even rednecks defer to a Pizza Mobile, believing that the Pizza Guy has much less to live for than they do. Unfortunately, I grew used to the way people drove defensively around me and thus just about killed myself a dozen times when off duty and driving without the bubble.

It also occurred to me that the scamming of drivers is the absolute cornerstone of the national pizza empire. You see, they offer drivers a flat rate for fuel per run — usually between 50 and 75 cents. The drivers, mostly guys in serious need of cash, gloss over this fact, thinking about the mythical $5 tip lurking behind the next door. The $5 tip almost never materializes, but the ten-mile round trip with the $1 tip often does. Guess what? At that rate, the driver is *paying* for the privilege of delivering the pizza. I mean, even the IRS, the stingiest bastards on the planet, admit it costs between 35 and 50 cents per mile to operate a vehicle . . . because the IRS is forced to take into account fuel, oil, maintenance, and insurance. If a driver makes a ten-mile round-tripper, he's got to get a $2.50 tip to break even! In reality, he's fueling and maintaining his car in order to deliver pizza, in order to fuel and maintain his car, in order to deliver pizza, and so on.

The corporate gurus know this, as surely as pizza makes you fat. But they carry forward with the policy, because to change from this system — and actually reward the drivers fairly for their work — would take money out of the fat-cat franchisee's pocket. The corporate solution, of course, is based on the law of supply and demand: as long as there are guys with a low *supply* of cash, we'll *demand* they take a screwing . . . and if they don't like it, they can quit.

Which, of course, I did.

Overall Analysis of the Job

When all was said and done, being a Pizza Guy is pretty cool. Why? The divine lack of client interaction. You get on your iron horse and deliver those pizza pies like a twenty-first-century Pony Express rider. It was the dream job for a guy like me, except for one thing: short hours plus rip-off driving policies times minimum wage minus taxes equals no actual income. If they'd been able to give me forty hours at a real income of eleven dollars an hour, I'd probably still be riding the iron horse. Come on . . . eleven dollars an hour for people to leave you alone? Sign me up.

In my case, the client interaction on the job was pretty mundane. No robberies, no deliveries to a crew filming a porn flick. I did, I suppose, have a couple of funny deliveries, like the poor lady who wanted to pay with a deposit slip instead of a check because of her concerns about identity theft . . . the guy asleep on his porch in front of the door, because he was afraid he was too drunk to hear the doorbell . . . and the classic stoner who needed to me to help him count his money because his fingers wouldn't work . . . all good stuff. For the most part, however, it was a relaxing, casual job.

Before closing this section about the pizza profession, however, a confession is in order. After the initial training session where I sat through pizza school with that merry band of misfits, I reported to work and never saw another weirdo. In fact, most of the guys who worked at my store were straight out of *Leave It to Beaver* and *Happy Days:* Eddie, Lumpy, Wally, Richie, Potsie, and Ralph, all present and accounted for . . . oh, and me, of course, in a cameo as the Fonz.

So, bottom line on the job? If you have evenings free from six to nine, don't need any extra money, and have a car that gets at least seventy-five miles to the gallon, give some thought to being a Pizza Guy. Just don't act on it.

We All Scream, Eventually

Deciding on my second bottom-rung job was easy. Why? Because my beautiful wife — who didn't need to lose an ounce — had gone Atkins on me. Atkins, in case you're a recent arrival from Mars, is a low-carbohydrate diet, which translates to a "no sugar . . . not even natural sugar" diet. What food groups have no sugar? Meat, cheese, and turnips. As a result, our cupboards were empty, and our refrigerator looked like a butcher shop in the Dutch town of Gouda. Yes, meat is good and I like cheese, but forcing down a fist-sized chunk of meat for your fifteenth consecutive meal is something only Eskimos are properly designed to handle. The bottom line was that I needed some sugar, and needed it bad. This led me to the tastiest source of sugar available, ice cream. My next professional endeavor would be as an Ice Cream Scooper Dude.

First, a little history on the topic. A Google for "History of Ice Cream" offered 26,126,789 matches.

Several minutes of clicking revealed that there are a number of myths and legends about the invention of ice cream — the most common of which is that the Chinese invented it and Marco Polo brought it back to Europe. Based on my reading of history, that brings the number of things "the Chinese invented and Marco Polo brought to Europe" to a grand total of . . . everything. If you believed *all* the Marco Polo stories, you'd have no choice but to believe the Europeans were dressed in leaves and gnawing on rocks for nutrition when Marco blew into town. Yes, Mr. Polo was an important explorer and to this day remains a great swimming pool game, but the ice cream myth is fudge-covered.

The reality of the situation is that no one knows when or where ice cream was actually invented. All the Web sites dance around the topic by talking about Roman emperors who poured syrup and fruit over snow and covert Italian-French connections and recipes, complete with King Charles I bribing his chef to keep secret the recipe for the new invention. None these theories is very satisfying intellectually, because even a four-year-old can figure out that snow would taste better with sugar on it . . . and the last time I checked, most European kings enforced their will via the threat of cranium removal, not a bribe for the cook.

As best we can tell, at some point between 1500 BC and 1500 AD, somebody somewhere invented ice cream, and at some point after 1500 European royalty started eating it and noting in their diaries how good it was. We know that several of the founding fathers of these United States of America were fans of ice cream and that Dolley Madison served it in the White House when her husband "Jemmy" was in the Oval Office. In 1846, a New Jersey gal named Nancy

Johnson invented the hand-crank ice cream maker, but The Man kept her down by failing to explain that she needed to patent the machine. This resulted in a man named Young patenting the invention 1848, which was acceptable to The Man because Mr. Young was, yes, a man. As a respectful nod to the woman he clearly stole the idea from, Mr. Young named "his" invention the Johnson Ice Cream Machine.

In the 1850s, Jacob Fussel opened America's first ice cream factories and made piles of dough; sadly, his family lacked the foresight to begin manufacturing spandex clothing for the full-figured woman the factories would create, but no one's perfect.

By 1904, ice cream was a common treat, and ice cream vendors at the St. Louis World's Fair took up way more than their fair share of space. Of course, being Americans, the visitors ate more than their fair share of ice cream. Apparently, this inspired the following conversation to take place between a waffle-making immigrant named Ernest Hamwi and the ice cream vendor next to him:

ICE CREAM VENDOR: Hey, Ernie . . . how are sales?

ERNEST: Terreeble! Everybody eating you ice cream! No goot for me!

ICE CREAM VENDOR: I told you waffles were history. Ice cream is the future!

ERNEST: My fadda and my granfadda make de' waffles! I'm a waffle man!

ICE CREAM VENDOR: Too bad . . . I'm rolling in money over here. I've sold so much I've got to close up for the day. I'm out of dishes.

ERNEST: Yeah? You look very happy. Why don't I make you even happier? I'm just a-gonna roll up dis waffle, walk over der, and shove it down your —

ICE CREAM VENDOR: Hey! Look at that rolled-up waffle! Man, I could put my ice cream in that! How much for ten waffles?

ERNEST: Waffles are a neekel . . . but deese are, uh, ice cream cones . . . dey a dime.

With the ice cream cone now invented, the treat was mobile, and thus Americans could stuff their faces anywhere. And stuff they do: based on national data, the average American eats twenty-three quarts of ice cream and frozen dairy treats per year . . . and seeing how last year I ate about one quart, that means you must be *really* packing it down. A few additional facts you might want to know are that the United States, of course, eats more ice cream than anyone else; Sunday is the biggest sales day for ice cream, with July being the biggest sales month. Little kids and old people eat the most ice cream; and the number one flavor by far is vanilla (which certainly helps explain why so many Americans are boring).

With my research done, it was now time to land a job. Surely scooping ice cream would be a good gig, low pay or not. After all, the Ice Cream Scooper Dude gets to stuff himself stupid on ice cream all day, and an ice cream parlor is a place of joy, right? What could possibly be difficult or negative about this job? I envisioned myself becoming Willy Wonka, whistling during work and maybe learning a magic trick or two to delight the children. I'd smile, and wink at the parents, and learn a little something about the simple pleasure of simply bringing pleasure to others. Yes, this job would bring out the Candy Man in me.

Of course, I'd never *been* an Ice Cream Scooper Dude before . . . and now realize my giddy outlook on this particular trade was not unlike that of a young man who joins the Marines, dreaming of a chance to serve in combat. It *sounds* exciting, but the fact is that war is hell . . . and it's a rare soul who survives mortal combat and wants to go back into the belly of that particular beast. During my time behind the ice cream counter, armed only with an ice cream scoop, the Candy Man inside me did not emerge. Not even close. In fact, within a couple of months my inner Candy(ass) Man was tackled, hog-tied, and bludgeoned to death by my inner Ax-Murder Man. That poor Candy Guy never had a chance.

So what happened? What's so bad about this job? What caused this descent into Double Mocha dementia? I tracked my downward spiral as it occurred and will retell it as fully as possible. The truth be known, however, Scooping the 'Scream is, indeed, like serving in combat . . . and only my fellow Waffle Cone Warriors will ever know the real horror.

Enlistment

Getting the job as an Ice Cream Scooper Dude was not difficult. First I surveyed the overall ice cream–scape of the region and ruled out the parlors that didn't look fun, fresh, and festive. The decision was made also to bag the stores that had uniforms, as neither my id nor my superego was willing to go from having worn a Marine's dress blue uniform to wearing a pink apron that read "I scream! You scream!" As much as I'd like to be more specific about my actual place of employment, there's just way too much stuff in this section that can get me sued. The less you are able to narrow down the location, the better.

In the end, one place stood out: a place that seemed friendly and cute, without too many customers crowding into its confined space. (I didn't, after all, want to work that hard.) I dressed in presentable clothes — khaki pants and a white button-down — and simply walked in. It was, by any standards, a warm and inviting place that swaddled the ice cream experience in its most idyllic light.

Upon entering the "shoppe," I encountered a tired-looking guy about ten years my senior scooping some 'scream for a couple of chunky gals in sweats. He looked tired, not like Shaq after a game but more like a POW coming home from war. Something inside his psyche had been rode hard and put up wet, and you could sense it in his movements. Eventually, the chunky gals waddled past me, eyeing their cones like a couple of TV lawyers watching a car wreck. I stepped up to the counter and asked the gentleman if he was the manager, and he replied that he was the owner.

"Wonderful. I'd like to apply for a job."

"A job?" he replied.

"Yes, sir."

"Did you just call me . . . sir?"

"Yes, sir."

"You're hired," he said. "When can you start?"

He heard the word "immediately" and told me I was hired immediately. No background checks, no social security number, no interview, and no chitchat. He asked for my driver's license, copied down the information, and guided me around behind the counter so he could start training me.

"I'm just curious," I asked. "Why did you hire me so quickly?" (In all fairness, one must bear in mind that my *not* really wanting the job emboldened me to ask questions a normal employee might not.)

"You didn't call me dude," he replied. "And your pants aren't falling down."

The training to be an Ice Cream Scooper Dude in a non-chain ice cream store is not very difficult, and because there aren't a bunch of goofy corporate procedures it's mostly intuitive. The owner simply explained how big a scoop was supposed to be (small); how to make a milkshake (easy); how to make a hot fudge sundae and a banana split (biggest profit margins); and how to work the cash register.

That was it.

"Is there a uniform?" I asked.

"Yes. You must wear a shirt and shoes," he said.

"Are there any benefits if I work full-time?"

"Yes," he said. "All the ice cream you can eat."

"How do you monitor inventory?" I asked. "This is a cash business, and I want to make sure there's never a misunderstanding about sales versus cash."

The guy looked at me with the sort of gratitude normally reserved for someone who rings your doorbell carrying a plywood check signed by Ed McMahon.

"I, uh . . . have a pretty complete system in place by using the weight of the ice cream," he said, which meant there was no system whatsoever. "I appreciate your asking, and I hope you'll let me know if any of the other employees ever try to rip me off."

If? Ever? Try? Note to self: people who believe in the inherent goodness of man should not open cash businesses.

A mere four hours later, I was alone in the shoppe. It was me, the cash register, and more ice cream than Homer Simpson could eat if he smoked up a pound of Willie Nelson's finest. If you've never been behind the counter of an ice cream shoppe, it's hard to describe the intoxicating feeling. Friend, *you* are the man. A customer wants a scoop of happiness? You're the hero. A customer wants a malted chocolate shake? *Extra thick, comin' up.* Some sprinkles on that? *Happy to do it . . . let me put a few extra on there, just because you've got such pretty eyes.* You are the God of the Good Stuff, and you want to give every customer a little scoop of heaven, served with a smile.

The place was empty that first hour, so I pretty much just poked around, refreshing myself on where the supplies were, gorging on the ice creams, and poking through cabinets and drawers to see if anyone left behind a copy of *Ice Cream Weekly.* I analyzed the layout of the place and wondered if there'd been any professional advice in its design. The shoppe was pretty small, so anyone with business sense has got to wonder if the cost of the square footage factored into the business plan pro forma. Because the shoppe fronted a shopping area, it occurred to me that perhaps a consultant recommended setting up a "get and go" business in order to maximize traffic flow with minimal overhead. Yes, much of that first hour was spent attempting to analyze the owner's overall business strategy. In retrospect, it is clear that my time would have been better spent analyzing when monkeys were going to fly out of my butt.

First Blood

My first solo customers were two overweight college girls in sweats, who waddled in giggling and talking about how this little adventure was going to blow their diet. It's hard to say what diet they were on, but it certainly wasn't one that included losing weight in the overall strategy.

"No worries!" I exclaimed. "Our ice cream is home-made, so that must mean it's good for you, right?"

More giggling as they looked through the glass.

"Can I try the Blueberry Cheesecake?" the one in pink asked.

"Try?" I replied.

"Yeah, y'all have those little pink spoons for tasting."

Some little pink spoons caught my eye. "Cool!" I said. "I didn't even know we had these. Sure, you can have a taste."

I scooped a little chunk and gave it to her.

"Hmm," she said, allowing the Blueberry Cheesecake ice cream to melt in her mouth. "That's good. How about the Banana Cream Pie?"

Another pink spoon, another little scoop.

"Yum," she said. "That's awesome. Can I try one more?"

"Of course!"

"How about the Heath Bar Mocha?"

"Sure," I said, and pink-spooned her again.

"Wow," she said. "I can't decide. Stephanie, you go."

Stephanie stepped up to the plate.

"Chocolate chip," she said. "Gimme a taste of that."

Done.

"How about the Lemon Custard?"

Done.

"Oh, and let me try . . . uh, Strawberry Cheesecake."

"What's the magic word?" I asked playfully, noticing that I'd dispensed six taster spoons and there'd been nary a single magic word.

Stephanie giggled. "Please?"

Done.

Time for the order. My first. Cash changes hands, and the Candy Man earns his keep. My heart raced.

"I'd like a single scoop of Double Fudge Chocolate," said Miss Pink Sweats.

"Double Fudge Chocolate?" I thought. "Those other flavors she tasted just must not have had the power to eclipse the divinity of our Double Fudge Chocolate." Note to self: remember that Double Fudge Chocolate is something special.

"Sugar cone, wafer cone, or cup?" I asked.

"Umm . . . let me think. Stephanie, you go."

"I'd like a single scoop of Mint Julep Chip," said Stephanie.

Again, note to self: she didn't go with any of the ones she tasted. Mint Julep Chip must also be something spectacular.

"Sugar cone, wafer cone, or cup?" I asked cheerfully.

"Cup," she said, and the scooping commenced. I leaned into the ice cream with my shoulder and formed a nice round ball like the one from training. Just before pulling it up out of the container, I scooped again, increasing the size of the ball. I wanted Stephanie to be happy and return frequently despite her dieting ways.

Plop. The ball of Mint Julep Chip dropped into the cup.

"You know what?" Stephanie queried.

"What?"

"I think I'd really rather have it in a cone."

"I understand. I like cones myself. They're more fun. Sugar cone or wafer cone?"

She turned to Miss Pink. "What are you getting?"

"Sugar cone, I think."

Stephanie turned back to me. "Sugar cone."

The ball of Mint Julep Chip nestled carefully into the sugar cone.

"Ta-dah!" I said, handing it to her across the stainless steel counter.

"Awww . . ." she said.

"Awww?"

"The other guy makes them bigger."

"The other guy?"

"Yeah, the tall guy. He makes them much bigger."

The "tall guy" must be a fellow employee, because the owner was a good three inches shorter than me.

"Well," I said, "I don't want to be the scrooge . . . Let me add some."

This was, of course, in direct violation of the size policy described by the owner, but imagine my horror at the prospect of short-creaming my customer . . . and the customer is always right, right? A good twenty-five percent more ice cream was scooped into the ball.

"Better?"

"I guess," Stephanie replied.

"Have you decided?" I asked Miss Pink.

"Yes, instead of the Double Fudge Chocolate I'd like the Peppermint Cookies and Cream."

"Sugar cone?"

"Okay."

"Ta-dah!" I said, and handed the cone across the counter. Without another word, Stephanie handed me exactly $4.23, and the two girls left giggling. No, they didn't thank me, but my job was done. The ladies were "coned" and gone, and the money was in the cash register. I was transformed into a worthy employee. And like a new-to-combat infantryman who walks away from his first skirmish unscathed, I was blissfully unaware of the horror that lurked within the details of that first customer encounter. My job was done and my pay was earned, and I'd lived to fight another day. My thousand-yard stare would come, sooner rather than later, but for the moment it all felt good.

Fields of Fire

The shoppe closed at 9:30 p.m., so around 9:00 I moved through the closeout procedures the owner had taught me. Sure, a few more customers might wander in, but due to my soaring confidence level, the idea of serving while closing seemed easy. I wiped the counters, stowed the condiments that needed refrigeration, carefully wiped the stainless steel between the ice cream buckets, washed all the dirty utensils, and sealed the hot fudge container. Yes, this was premature, because I was bound to do a little dripping while serving my final customers, but it seemed like a good plan: a little touch-up at 9:30, close out the cash register (called Zee-ing the register), hide the money, and clock out by 9:40. I do, however, remember thinking, "I wonder why we close at 9:30 and not 9:00?"

At 9:15, a couple of customers strolled in, chatting about the movie they'd just seen. It was a college-aged couple dressed in way too much black, both trying to appear aloof and cool, so it didn't surprise me when they didn't ask for little taster spoons of various flavors.

"Gimme a couple chocolate cones," said the guy.

The bins between us contained no less than four types of chocolate.

"Well," I said, "you've come to the right place for chocolate. We've got Double Fudge Chocolate, Marshmallow Chocolate, Chocolate Cookie Dough, and Chocolate Chocolate Chip."

"I just want regular chocolate," he said.

"The Double Fudge Chocolate is great," I said.

"Just regular chocolate."

I looked down into the bins. To my amazement, regular chocolate did not magically appear.

"I'm afraid those are the only kinds we have."

"What are they again?" he asked. He was unable to read the names of the ice creams for himself, because he was very slowly looking for something very important in his leather jacket pockets. I ran through the flavors, ensuring they sounded inviting in the way I pronounced them.

"I don't care," he said. "Elizabeth, what do you want?"

"I'd like the Chocolate Cookie Dough."

"Gnarly," he said. "You sure?"

At this moment I saw what I *hoped* was a hallucination brought on by the four pounds of ice cream in my stomach: it appeared to be a banzai charge of Dr. Seuss characters, all of whom were streaming into the shoppe. They were short and tall, lean and fat, there was even a goth, in a stupid top hat. It wasn't, however, a vision. Fonzie and his girlfriend weren't the only ones who'd been to the movies, and these were the other attendees who were choosing ice cream over cigarettes and brandy to end their evening. The thought of all those customers unsettled me, so I ignored the throng streaming in the door and focused my attention on Fonzie and his girlfriend.

". . . yeah, but Cookie Dough?" the guy said. "How third grade is that?"

"Just let me order what I want! I want Cookie Dough!" the girl shot back, sounding more like someone on her way home from arts and crafts than an art film.

"That's cool . . . chill!" the guy said, ensuring there would be no sex that night. "Gimme one Chocolate Cookie Dough and one of those Fudge Chocolate ones."

"Sugar cone, wafer cone, or cup?"

"Whatever."

Important Sidebar: I was once in a conversation that included two Marine buddies and my wife, during which we discussed the word/expression "Whatever." One of my buddies explained that he and his wife had had a similar conversation after she'd used the word/expression, and he told her to never use it again. His wife insisted he explain why it was such a big deal. "Because," my buddy explained, "what you're really saying is F —— you." His point was and is completely valid and has instilled in me a strong aversion to the word/expression. Just ask my wife. End of note.

"So a cup will be okay?"

"Yeah," Fonzie replied.

"Can I get a cone?" Elizabeth asked, as the crowd of Dr. Seuss characters began to press in around them.

"Sure! Sugar cone, or wafer cone?"

"If you get a cone, you'll drip in the Beemer," Fonzie said.

"Todd, I want a cone, and I'm getting a cone," she said. "Please, please, please just shut the hell up."

"Sugar or wafer?" I added cheerfully.

Plop, plop, $4.23. Gone.

The crowd pressed in.

A few moments arose during the next hour when Persians attempted to overwhelm this lone Spartan, but for the most part it was fun. Everyone packed into the shoppe rec-

ognized the obvious, which is one employee + lots of customers = customers milling around jonesing. Fortunately,
this inspired most of them to have their order in mind when
they got to the counter. Plop, plop, plop, it ran mostly like
clockwork. Sure, a couple of yo-yos ordered milkshakes,
and one guy ordered a banana split, but when everyone
around the banana split guy groaned, he changed his order
to a triple scoop and asked if he could just have a banana. I
told him he could, because I was powerful and generous.
All in all, it was mostly a controlled chaos, exacerbated by
my inexperience, but everyone eventually got their goods,
and all hands left happy.

When the register was Zee'ed out at 10:30, it felt like a
good day's work. The next day was Saturday, and the
schedule demanded my presence from 3:00 until 11:00.
My coworker would be Ronnie, a three-year veteran of the
ice cream wars.

Walking Point

Upon my arrival at 2:50 the next day, Ronnie had been on
duty for three hours.

" 'Sup, bro!" he said as I came around the counter.
"You the new guy?"

Ronnie was a burly guy of around twenty, with red
curly hair and a goatee. He wore a backwards baseball
cap, a jersey of some sort (size XXXXXL), and of course
his pants were practically around his ankles. He had that

still-buzzed-from-the-night-before air about him, and he used his hands when he talked like those rap music guys. As best I can recall, our initial conversation went pretty much like this:

"Are you Ronnie? I'm Prioleau Alexander."

"Pray what?"

"Pray-low."

"Not anymore, dude," Ronnie said. "You need an ice cream name. And your ice cream name is . . . Banana Man. You can call me Chilly."

"Your name is a lot cooler than mine," I said.

"I'm the senior jerk," he said.

"Jerk?"

"Yeah, like the olden days. The soda jerks that worked the fountains, man. We're jerks, for short. I'm the senior jerk, so I get to give out the names."

"How many of us are there?"

"Five, plus Mr. Darnell, the owner. Three dudes — you, me, and Dr. Pepper, and two chicks — Creamy and Whipping."

I nodded.

"Why you workin' a lousy job like this?" Chilly asked.

"Just need the work," I said.

"How come you're not doing a tie job or something? You look all proper to me."

"Nah, not anymore. Taking a break."

"You think this is takin' a break?"

"Maybe."

"You ain't worked a Saturday," Chilly said, and promptly snapped open his cell phone to place a call. I'd served twenty customers and been on the clock an hour when he hung up.

"Okay, Banana Man," Chilly said, "take five. I'll front the booth."

"Chilly," I said, "this doesn't seem like much of a two-man operation. Why are we both on the clock?"

"You never know about Saturdays," he said. "Sometimes we get waves of people. I think it's got something to do with the moon or something."

"The moon?"

"Yeah, you've seen all that research about how girls get horny during the full moon, and serial killers get all Jack the Ripper? You know, like that. But it makes them eat ice cream, I think. Saturdays are weird sometimes."

"Is this one of those Saturdays?"

"Nah. We'd have felt it by now . . . people comin' in all famished. You'd know."

"Should one of us go home? To save Mr. Darnell some money?"

"Not allowed. He sets the schedule, and we scoop the 'scream. I'm off at six, though, so you'll be walking point solo."

I nodded.

"Today's your second day?"

I nodded again.

"You hate it yet?"

"No, I had fun last night."

"You ain't hit five thousand pinks yet. You'll hate it then."

"Five thousand pinks?"

"Yeah . . . about the five thousandth time you've used those little pink spoons to give someone a taste of an ice cream they ain't gonna buy, you'll snap. You'll be all like, 'Order some ice cream, ya freakin' moose!' After you snap on *that* one, it only gets worse. Then it gets *really* bad."

Chilly laughed.

The Average Day

Here is how your day would unfold, if you were dumb enough to be me: You'd start your shift by either opening the store, or getting a handoff from someone else. Opening the store is a pretty simple process, simply because there are no corporate policies to follow. In fact, here's a complete list of your opening procedures: Turn on the lights. The store is now open. Get the cash out from under the counter, and make sure there is twenty-five dollars in change and small bills. The store is now ready for business.

Unless you had a customer follow you in, you'd take the first couple of minutes to scan for new Post-its from Mr. Darnell. Post-its, you quickly learn, are Mr. Darnell's way of communicating new policies and procedures, which usually came to him when he realized some basic task his lazy employees were failing to accomplish. Among the permanently displayed Post-its would be these nuggets of wisdom: *Acknowledge the customer immediately! Wash this milkshake machine! Refill napkin holders when they are empty! Use soap when washing your hands! You must clock in AND out!*

Chances are you have an IQ above 35, so these notes might just as well say: *Remember to inhale AND exhale! Keep your eyes moist by blinking! Put ice cream in the ice cream cone!* But as a new employee, you'd understand the need for these Post-its, and you'd probably feel sorry for Mr. Darnell for needing them. Like me, you'd doubt seriously Mr. and Mrs. Darnell had any idea what they were getting into when they mortgaged the house to start a business that required student-age labor.

After scanning for Post-its, you would take care of the things the person closing the night before had blown off, like *Washing the milkshake machine!* and *Refilling the napkin holder!* This exhaustive process would take you entire minutes, and upon concluding it you would . . . do . . . nothing.

Observing the Enemy

Here's the thing, and I'll tell you in advance: Chilly was right. Around 5,000 pinks, give or take, you snap.

But in the meantime, you're living on a slippery slope, and you notice a lot of things on the slide down.

Take, for instance, the customers. You may not be aware of this, but seventy-five percent of the people who walk into an ice cream parlor *need* to be walking, just not into an ice cream shoppe. You don't notice this at first, because you're focusing on bringing joy to people, but eventually you can't help it. You begin to think less about the fact you're giving them joy and more about the fact you're giving them a near-future heart attack. Not everyone is overweight, of course, but they do tend to fall into some fairly standard subgroups. Here's a look at the most frequent patron groups:

The College Girls: This subgroup arrives usually in sweats, carrying with them an extra thirty-five pounds. These are the gigglers, who laugh about their diets, and always associate their trip to the trough with some sort of well-deserved reward. There's talk of the test they just took, or the stress they've been under, or the fact they've recently lost ten pounds. They never, and I mean *never,* come alone . . . I think that's because they want their friends to gain the same weight they do. (It's not unlike when cokeheads share their coke . . . Everyone wants company on the hell-bound express.) There's also another interesting phenomenon that occurs with these gals. You know how a good-looking chick always has a couple hefty friends with her when she's out clubbing and attracting attention? Well, the gals on Team Ice Cream don't return the favor, and the cute one doesn't make the cut when they rally the troops for an assault on Mount Syrup-bachi.

The Beautiful People: You'd be surprised at the number of beautiful people who come into an ice cream shoppe. Now, please understand, it's not "beautiful people" in the derogatory sense . . . These are people who are physically beautiful, complete with sculpted abs, defined arms, and that irritating way of looking good after an eight-mile run.

Of all the groups I came to hate, this group inspired the least hate, mostly because they were all business when they came in. Most had a specific flavor they wanted, and they didn't need to torture me with the tales of why they deserved to treat themselves. When you do four thousand ab crunches a day, you get to eat what you want . . . and the loser behind the ice cream counter hardly deserves an explanation. The beautiful people didn't mind being in the shoppe with the college girls, but the college girls hated being in the shoppe with them. As a result, the line-deferment ritual was fascinating, and went like this: Two college girls are doing their fifth pink spoon each, and a beautiful couple walks in. Like two lionesses caught gorging on a downed giraffe, the college girls turn to confront the interlopers. Eye contact is made, and body mass data is exchanged. The tension becomes thick. One, two, three: "You two go ahead," one of the college girls would say, "we haven't decided yet." The giggling ceases and the conversation stops until the beautiful couple is gone. The ritual resumes. Back to that giraffe.

The Suffering Dad: I must confess that my heart went out to this long-suffering demographic for longer than it should have. Why? Because they came into the shoppe with such good intentions. All they wanted was to give their kids some inexpensive joy, and they really, really tried to stop the kids from torturing me. This was impossible, of course, but they did their best. Here is my best attempt to recreate the Suffering Dad scenario:

DAD: Okay, kids! Who wants ice cream!

KIDS 1–3: Me! Me! Me!

KID 1: I wanna try the Banana kind!

KID 2: Me too!

KID 3: I wanna try the Bubblegum!

KID 2: Yeah, I mean, that's what I want!

DAD: Everyone can try one flavor, but that's it . . . Sorry about this.

ME: No problem. Happy to help.

KID 1: Banana! Banana!

ME: Here you go, sport.

KID 1: Mmmm. That's not that good. Dad, can I try one more?

DAD: No, son. It's William's turn.

KID 2: I want to taste Bubblegum.

DAD: You had Bubblegum last time. You know what it tastes like.

KID 2: I can't remember.

DAD: (Sigh.)

ME: Here you go, little fellow.

KID 2: Mmmm. That doesn't taste like last time. Dad, can I try the Banana?

DAD: Michael just tried the Banana, and said it wasn't that good.

KID 2: But what if he's just being a fart face?

Note: Let me fast-forward here by about three minutes. My post-traumatic stress disorder is starting to flare up, and I need to move on. So . . . three minutes later.

DAD: Do you want a spanking?!! I'll pull your pants down right here and give you a spanking. Go sit in the car with your brother. Right now! Sorry about all this . . . Give me three scoops of vanilla in cups. God . . . how can these children be mine? You got kids?

ME: *(Plop, plop, plop)* No, sir.

DAD: You're a genius. You shouldn't be working here — you should be at a think tank, or at NASA or something. Anyone smart enough to not have kids should be the frickin' president.

ME: That's $6.34, unless you'd like something for yourself.

DAD: For me? How about a gun? You got a *gun?*

The Suffering Dad mixes with all other ice cream patrons equally, which is to say he is mortified no matter who is watching.

The Towel Throwers: This delightful subgroup consists of the 300-plus-pounders, who've simply thrown in the towel on the idea that any sort of moderation matters. Like the Suffering Dads, this is a group you feel sorry for until you come to hate them. Sometimes alone, and sometimes in pairs, the Towel Throwers waddle into the shoppe as if it's a doctor's visit and they've come to reluctantly take their medicine. If the Towel Throwers have a redeeming feature, it's that they no longer bother with the pink spoons — it's all or nothing. Their orders are rarely preceded by any conversation or attempts at justification, and through their breathless panting you hear only, "One scoop Mocha Chocolate Chip, one scoop Cherry Chocolate Swirl . . . in a cup. And a large Mountain Dew." I can honestly say that I'd probably have more zeal in my voice ordering "One tetanus shot, and an ingrown toenail removal."

The group dynamics with the Towel Throwers are, however, extremely interesting. First, there's the College Girls vs. the Towel Throwers. The Towel Throwers don't notice the College Girls, but boy-oh-boy do the College Girls notice them. Through endless hours of observation, I deduced that the College Girls were both repulsed by and attracted to the Towel Throwers. Why? They are repulsed, because they see themselves five years hence unless something changes. They are attracted, however, because the Towel Throwers live in a state of blissful blubber, where even a peanut butter, bacon, and mayonnaise sandwich with a twelve-Zinger dessert is within reasonable consumption. To the College Girls, the Towel Throwers live a wonderful life in a mythical Krispy Kreme Kingdom, where éclairs are king and whipped crème is queen, and every human delight but sex is achievable. Repulsion, and attraction . . . I get the shivers thinking about it.

The Towel Throwers vs. the Beautiful People is far more hostile, as neither has much desire to acknowledge the other's presence. By being in the same room, especially when ordering ice cream, the Towel Throwers are reminded how unfair it is that they have "slow metabolism" and "low blood sugar." This usually results in an extra scoop to reduce the sting. The Beautiful People, however, are reminded of their own mortality, which usually cripples their appetite, and results in an order of a Diet Coke and God only knows how many extra ab crunches before bed. On more than one occasion we lost customers when one group saw the other before opening the front door.

The Towel Throwers and the Suffering Dads are, for the most part, birds of a feather and seem to mix nicely. Both wonder why God has sentenced them to their current life, and neither would object too terribly much if upon exiting the shoppe they were to be run over by a cement truck. Occasionally you would see horror on a Suffering Dad's face when he realized how rich the environment was for his kids to make a "fat" comment, but I never heard one myself.

Chilly swore that one time he was working a shift and a Towel Thrower at the counter had her beeper go off. The kid behind her said to his Suffering Dad, "Watch out, Dad. She's backing up." For what it's worth, I don't believe Chilly actually saw this: it sounds like an urban myth to me.

The Ear Touchers: The final standard group who frequented my shoppe was the Ear Touchers. The Ear Touchers were the women who obviously didn't work, except to disprove the old saying "A woman can never be too rich, too thin, or too tan." Whipping was the one who actually gave them the name, because she said that they'd all continue to get face-lifts until their ears touched. The Ear Touchers were famous for what a rush they always pretended to be in . . . as if they were on the way to help the police negotiate a hostage crisis that had broken out at a book club. With Ear Touchers, it was always a single scoop in a cup. Always. I asked Whipping why this was, and she said it was so they'd have a container to purge it back up into.

There was also almost no interaction between the Ear Touchers and the other groups, mostly because the Ear Touchers had a body language and a system of distractions that enabled them to ignore everyone. Obviously their preference was to rush in and rush out with no one getting in their very important way. If this mission proves impossible, and they do get stuck in line, their first line of antisocializing defense is their cell phone. They whip it out of their fifty-five-gallon purse, speed-dial a number, and have a hushed conversation with someone important — who knows, maybe their tanning booth towel boy. Following the phone call, the next move is to bull their way to the front to survey the choices in order to prepare themselves for the moment of truth. (This often caused tension between them and the Towel Throwers, as the Towel Throwers would panic inwardly until the Ear Toucher was back in her proper place in the line.) If the Ear Toucher was still in line post-decision, the next move was the one that would see them through to the ordering process: audible siiiigh, check Rolex for time, remove magazine from purse, and pretend to be engrossed in some very important article. Ear Touchers are always far more comfortable in pairs, as a wait in line simply offers them a chance to discuss (in the presence of us unwashed folks) the vast sums they pay each month for maid service. For some reason, it was the Ear Touchers I came to hate the most, probably because they stood in such ugly contrast to my wife, who didn't mind a bit that her husband was a full-time ice cream scooper. For an Ear Toucher, admitting your husband was an Ice Cream Scooper Dude would be the eleventh circle of hell.

Probing the Defensive Perimeter

Slowly but surely, life as an Ice Cream Scooper Dude became combat. Sure, it wasn't easy to admit to myself for a while, but the truth was that Chilly, Doc, Creamy, and Whipping were all engaged in a raging firefight, and I was there as a conscientious objector. I was trying to convince myself that scooping the 'scream was good. It was fun. It was certainly better than being in advertising . . . but in the end, my faux-cheerful attitude got sucked into the hellish inferno of the Waffle Cone Wars like a Reese's Piece through a Towel Thrower's straw. Why? What dragged me into the fray?

It was all the *defensive perimeter probing.* Over and over and over they probed. Eventually, they found my weaknesses, then pounded those weaknesses day after day after day. And then, snap! And yes, it was right around 5,000 pinks.

It was, in fact, those little pink spoons that carved the first chink in my perimeter. Let me tell you why, by first giving an example of a scenario between you and me, where both of us have manners:

ME: Hi, there.
YOU: Hi. *(You inspect the ice cream selection.)* You know, I think the Banana Fudge Royale sounds good, but I've never had it before. Can I have a little scoop to see if I like it?
ME: Sure.
YOU: *(You taste.)* Wow, that is good. Could I have a scoop of that in a cup?
ME: Sure. *(Plop.)*

YOU: Have a good one.

ME: Thank you. Come see us again soon.

Now, I ask you: Is that hard? Is there anything about that encounter that makes you feel uncomfortable? Do you feel less important being polite, and using the pink spoon for its actual purpose? Didn't think so. Now, let me formulate the average pink spoon encounter between you and, say, a College Girl:

YOU: Hi, there.

GIRL: *(No eye contact, as her beady eyes scan the trough)* I wanna try that M&M Vanilla.

YOU: There you go.

GIRL: *(Before the ice cream has even registered with her taste buds)* Lemme try the Coffee Peppermint.

YOU: There you go.

GIRL: *(Her head is now swaying back and forth, like a grizzly looking into a stream for spawning salmon.)* Snickers Crunch.

YOU: There you go.

GIRL: *(More swaying)* Mocha Swirl.

YOU: There you go.

GIRL: I'll take a scoop of Cookies and Cream.

YOU: Sugar cone, wafer cone, cup, or should I just shove it down your pie hole?

Okay, so you might not say that, but reread that encounter. Envision it in your mind. Then replay it twelve hundred times (because that puts you around five thousand pinks). No eye contact twelve hundred times. No please twelve hundred times. No thank you twelve hundred times. Never order a scoop of what you sampled twelve hundred times. It is enough to drive you to be a jerk, and not the soda-pulling kind.

Next weakness? The fact that asking, "Sugar cone, wafer cone, or cup?" as a part of *every* order began to drive me insane.

Is this a reasonable gripe? You probably think not. You think it wouldn't bother you. But after you've been there for 5,000 pinks, reality would set in: dozens of times a day you serve two or three friends standing together, and after the first person orders you say, "Sugar cone, wafer cone, or cup?" Hint to next two friends . . . Guess what the options are!??

MARY: I'd like the Chocolate Bean.
YOU: Sugar cone, wafer cone, or cup?
MARY: Ummmmmmmmmmmmmmmmmmmmmmm . . . cup.
YOU: And you?
JIM: Carmel Crunch.
YOU: *(Silent pause)* Sugar cone, wafer cone, or cup?
JIM: Ummmmmmmmmmmmmmmmmmmmmmm . . . cone.
YOU: Sugar cone or wafer cone?
JIM: Sugar cone.
YOU: And you?
MARTHA: Pralines and Cream.
YOU: Sugar cone, wafer cone, or cup?
MARTHA: What's a sugar cone?

Imagine asking the same question over and over and over and over and over, and no one *ever* anticipating it. Not the regulars, not the groups, not the people from the shop next door . . . no frickin' one. Ever. It's like some kind of reverse, verbal Chinese water torture.

It was a Sunday afternoon when I was teamed with Creamy that I admitted the enemy was taking its toll. Creamy was a cute, dirty-blonde gal who enrolled in the local college to study political science and seemed way too smart to be sitting in an ice cream parlor for extra cash. I'd just pink-spooned four College Girls and asked "the question" four times in a row. When they left, I struck up a conversation with Creamy, who was immersed in a hot fudge sundae.

ME: Creamy, how long have you been working here?
CREAMY: A year.
ME: How do you like it?
CREAMY: It sucks.
ME: Why?
CREAMY: Because I hate all the customers.
ME: Why is that?
CREAMY: You've been here a month . . . you hate 'em all too. You tell me.
ME: Can you tell I hate everyone?
CREAMY: Nah, you do a pretty good job of hiding it. But no one can be here more than a month and not hate it. What do you hate the worst?
ME: The pinks. It's driving me crazy.
CREAMY: Wait until you've been here a year.
ME: How do you take it?

CREAMY: My boyfriend gave me good advice. He said, "You learn to love the rope."

ME: What?

CREAMY: He was telling me about this movie, where they had a Vietnam POW and someone asked him how he could take the rope torture they used all the time. The POW said, "You learn to *love* the *rope* . . . Then you're beating them, and they don't even know it."

ME: How do you learn to love the rope?

CREAMY: You'll learn. Or you'll quit.

ME: I'm curious . . . Does your boyfriend call you Creamy?

CREAMY: Sure . . . when he's in the mood to not have sex for a few days.

The Jerk Squad

As I mentioned, one of the reasons for writing this book is the question, "Who are the people who work these jobs?" Let me take a moment to run through our starting lineup.

Chilly, the senior jerk, remained pretty much an enigma to me, as are all the kids of his generation. His name was Ronnie, and he lived in a mobile home community ("a freakin' trailer park," in his words) on the edge of the city. He'd moved out of his parents' home the day after high school graduation and moved to town with a high school buddy in order to "bag some college chicks," a large number of whom lived in cookie-cutter apartments near his mobile home. A great number of the college's male students also lived in Chilly's mobile home community, but Chilly refused to befriend any of them. They were, he said, "a bunch of momma's boys who had everything handed to them on a silver platter." I've never thought of a trailer park as a place where a great deal of silverware was stored, but Chilly felt otherwise. I asked him if being buddies with some of the college guys wouldn't get him invited to parties where the college chicks were, but he said it wasn't necessary. "If there's a party I want to go to, I just crash," he said. "Nobody's gonna mess with me. You don't mess with the guy who cuts your hair, mixes your drinks, or scoops your ice cream."

I tried a couple times to find out from Chilly where he felt his life was headed, but the concept just wasn't on his radar screen. It was during one of these attempts that Chilly explained to me that he and four other buddies had formed a group called the Poets. The word "Poets" stood for "Piss On Everything, Tomorrow Sucks." From what I could surmise, the Poets' primary function was to *ensure* tomorrow sucked. Chilly explained to me one of the Poets' rules. "It goes like this," he said. "If two Poets show up together at a third Poet's house, the third guy has to go out drinking with them. No excuses. Last Thanksgiving, we nabbed one guy who was walking out to his car to go eat with his parents. He had to call his folks from a strip joint. Man, that was freakin' hilarious."

In Chilly's mind, the ice cream job was a pretty good gig. His first job upon moving to town had been roofing, which he described as "the worst freakin' job in the world." When he discovered he could make almost the same money "chillin' behind an ice cream counter," he leapt at the chance. In honor of his good fortune, he'd changed his ice cream name to Chilly upon attaining the vaunted rank of senior jerk. As for his performance at work, he was the best of all of us, because he was the only one who worked the job full-time and didn't pray at night he'd get fired. Yes, he hated it too . . . but he'd been a roofer, and he swore that until you've been a roofer, you don't really know the meaning of "This job sucks."

I asked Chilly once if he was planning to go to college.

"College," he said, "is for losers."

Creamy, the dirty blonde I spoke of earlier, was an archetypical "cute college girl" from Jacksonville, Florida. Her real name was Leslie, and she was scooping the 'scream because her parents felt working was a character-building thing and shorted her monthly money needs by a couple hundred bucks to ensure she went out and built some character. I asked her one shift why she was scooping 'scream instead of bartending or waitressing, and she replied, "Banana, this is a college town, and all the bars are student bars. When you were in college, did you tip? No, you drank yourself stupid and breathed your cigarette breath all over the waitress trying to get her to go home with you. That's not a job; it's hell, with crappy lighting."

Creamy was a member of a sorority, and lots of her sisters would stop in to chat while she was on duty. Theirs was a fairly mature group of gals, very few of whom squealed or said, "Ohmahgawd." They were into the no makeup and hair preparation thing and the semi-crunchy approach to clothes. You know, gypsy skirts and T-shirts and floppy sweaters that looked comfortable. (Think Jodie Foster in

college.) This was in sharp contrast, however, to the lipstick
and hairspray sororities, whose members felt it was necessary to shriek, giggle, or grab someone in order to commu-
nicate any thought more complex than "Sugar cone."
(Think Jenna Bush in college.) As I got to know Creamy a
little better by working a few shifts with her, I came to realize the underlying seriousness came from an underlying
liberalness — a youthful concern about politics and world
events that hadn't yet been taxed out of her, or at least soft-
ened by a couple of decades of watching politicians make
teary-eyed confessions about intern non-sex. Creamy spent
more time working for the Democratic Party than I spent
working (period) in college.

I am fairly certain Creamy will do well in life. She'll get
out of college and quickly realize that being a political sci-
entist pays less than other professions, and she'll drift into
something like pharmaceutical sales (where they'll hire her
not because she's cute, but because her political science
degree makes her *more qualified* than the hundreds of unat-
tractive, unemployed pharmaceutical degree holders). Four
years, tops, and she'll be married to a doctor and living in a
gated community with tennis courts. From there, she'll join
the Junior League, have a couple kids, and after six years of
paying private school tuition, she'll find herself pulling the
Republican lever on Election Day. (Creamy, if you're out
there, and I'm wrong, please write and tell me . . . If you're
building playgrounds in Third World countries, I want to
retract the previous paragraph.) As for her work habits and
attitude, her performance was scary. She hated that job
worse than anyone, but her act was so convincing you'd

have thought she was retrieving every scoop for a member of the Kennedy family. Inside was a Fredericka Kruger, ready to slash your throat for asking for a cup of water, but on the outside was a sweet, fun-loving Ice Cream Scooper Chick. (Creamy's husband, if you're out there you be good, or learn to sleep with one eye open. You'll never know when it's coming.)

Dr. Pepper, aka Doc, was a real piece of work. Named Nathaniel by his parents, Doc was a life of tragedy in the making. His real problem, I think, was massive ADD. If his girlfriend told me he'd started sending text messages on his cell phone mid-coitus, I would have just shrugged. Unfortunately, Doc found at about age twenty-four that cocaine magically enhanced his ability to focus, and it turned out he really, really liked to focus. He focused his way through all of his money, his car, and his parents' antique hutch before ending up in rehab for the first time. Fortunately, Doc's parents were wealthy, so he received the best rehab care available . . . three times. His latest stint at the fuzzy slippers club had been at an inpatient joint in Michigan, where he got a therapist nine years his senior pregnant.

At the time we worked together, Doc was clean and sober and living with his folks. He worked at the shoppe as part of his ongoing rehab, which he said his parents felt was a "major accomplishment." Clearly he didn't share their excitement, as he once told me, "How pathetic is that? My own parents are excited I can scoop ice cream and not get fired. Can you imagine going home from this job and having your folks tell you how proud they are of you? Damn, dude, I'm a screw-up, not a Special Olympian."

Doc's downward spiral in life was a real shame, because he was one of the funniest, nicest, most upbeat people I'd ever met. His work behind the counter ranked as a Robin Williams–level performance, complete with shouts of praise for himself and good-natured mockery of the customers. He once told a little boy that he wouldn't scoop his ice cream unless the kid apologized to his dad and went out on the sidewalk and yelled, "My dad is the king." To emphasize the point, Doc scooped himself a cone of what the kid wanted and ate it. The kid complied, and the dad tipped Doc five bucks. Unfortunately, we never got to be friends outside work, because he was obliged to go home when he wasn't at work (a probationary requirement).

After leaving the ice cream world, I wondered about Doc from time to time and hoped he was doing well. One day, an email arrived from Mr. Darnell with an attached story from the weekly newspaper's police blotter. It told the sad tale of a "local man" who'd gone over to an ex-girlfriend's house at 2:00 a.m. and rung the doorbell for several minutes. Seeing her car in the driveway, the man scaled the home's latticework clear to the third floor. Through the window the man saw his ex "in the company of another man" and in a fit of passion head-butted his way through the closed window. When the police arrived, they found the woman and the other man barricaded in the bathroom, with the defendant dripping in blood, seated at the kitchen table eating cereal. The email was signed simply, "I don't think Dr. Pepper will be in to work this week."

The final member of the Jerk Crew was Whipping, known to the rest of the world as Laura. Whipping was a petite, cute college gal, who reminded you of a diminutive Gwyneth Paltrow almost immediately. I never got to know Whipping very well, primarily because she was very soft-spoken, and thus conversation with her felt like the *Seinfeld* episode about the low-talker. I did manage to discover her folks were wealthy, and she worked because she'd always worked. Whipping refused to acknowledge her ice cream name, claiming it was a product of Chilly's warped brain (duh), and refused to admit her disdain for the job like Chilly, Creamy, and me. Certainly Whipping *had* a personality, it just didn't show through that much at work. When someone would come in the shoppe, she'd stand there in a perfectly comfortable silence . . . unfazed by the fact that the customer was failing to acknowledge her. When they'd order, she'd simply nod her head, scoop the ice cream, and put it on a sugar cone without asking the horrid question. Unbelievably, ninety percent of her customers just took it, with nary a comment — and those who did object were folks wanting it in a cup. I tried this trick myself, and seventy percent of *my* customers corrected me and demanded their scoop be transferred to the wafer cone or the cup. How she was able to pull this off was a mystery to the rest of the crew . . . but she did. It was kind of like those kung-fu guys who can break boards with their tongue: she'd just channel her will into the customer, and the customer found him/herself unable to act like a dolt.

Perhaps the thing that shocked me the most about Whipping was disclosed on our last day of work together. She looked a little tired, and I asked her if she was feeling okay. She said she was, but that she was exhausted . . . She'd "hooked up" at a bar the night before, and it had been "a pretty wild night."

"Really?" I blurted, wondering if it was one of the guys who'd picked her up from work. Curiosity got the best of me, and I asked, "Did you know the guy?"

"Nah," she said, waited two beats, and added, "And it wasn't a guy."

The Thousand-Yard Stare

Among combat veterans, there is a thing called the thousand-yard stare. It comes with the sight of too much horror, too much death. It is called the thousand-yard stare because of the look that creeps into the eyes of some of these warriors: they seem to see everything and nothing simultaneously. They are looking out to a place they can't see . . . for something that doesn't exist.

My thousand-scoop stare arrived after one month and fourteen days of thirty-five hours a week. I'm embarrassed about careening over the edge so quickly, but the very nature of the business was my weakness: there was just way too much face time with clients, and it reminded me too much of life in the white-collar world.

I struggle for an explanation as to why the job broke me at all. I mean, the sole requirement for being a good jerk is being nice to people who aren't necessarily being nice to me. How hard is that? Hell, after fourteen years of being downright obsequious to people I wanted to sand-

wich in a waffle iron, you'd think that being polite to someone for sixty seconds would be easy. There is no decent
answer. Perhaps the six-hour shifts of scooping joy were too
long. Perhaps it's the salary associated with scooping the
'scream, which is $6.25 an hour before taxes; it haunted me
that in my position as an agency creative director, my time
was billed to the client for $6.25 every three minutes. But
whose fault is that? Whose fault is it that I was working a
bottom-rung job, instead of fake laughing at a client's jokes
for twenty times that amount?

I told Mr. Darnell it was time to move on, and he was
very concerned that he'd made me mad or somehow failed to
follow up on some preemployment promise of advancement.
A little embarrassed by the emotional trauma he was experi-
encing, I said, "Mr. Darnell, this is a great place to work.
You'll have me replaced by the end of the day."

"Yeah," he said, "but it was so nice to have an employee
who didn't call me dude in front of the customers."

"And my pants stay up," I added.

"Don't remind me," he said. "I get depressed thinking
about it."

Why the Roofer Wants
to Kick Your Ass

My next step into the working world was the only thing that even came close to the pain one endures in a Marine Corps training environment: I was a laborer with a construction company.

If you're like me, you've probably wondered why there are so many construction-worker bar/diner/dives where you aren't welcome. You wander into one of these places looking for a beer or a burger (with your tie loosened, of course), and there you find clusters of dirty, bruised men smoking cigarettes and peering at you like you're wearing a T-shirt that says, "NASCAR sucks." You look around, and it occurs to you that half the patrons limp, and everyone has tattoos. The overall atmosphere of the place chills several degrees with your very presence.

"What's the problem with these dirtbags?" you think. "Is there anyone in here who *doesn't* want to kick my ass?"

As a matter of fact, no — there isn't. The only thing keeping your butt unkicked is the cost of bail and the reality of lost wages.

Why is this?

You're a nice person, right? You go to work, you bust your butt for a living, you pay the bills, you drive a Chevy. What gives?

You need to back up. It's the "bust your butt for a living" thing.

You bust your *brain*, but you most assuredly do not bust your *butt*. Construction workers bust their butt. And because you *don't* bust your butt but *think* you bust your butt, this generates their desire to kick said butt. In fact, just having quit being a construction worker, I want to kick your ass.

The Demolition Man

I became a laborer by answering an ad on a grocery store bulletin board.

I showed up at a job site where a home was being built in the suburbs of Charleston, South Carolina, tracked down someone who looked like he spoke English, and asked him about the job. It was a typical summer day in Charleston, which is to say it was so hot that even the Channel 5 weatherman was at a loss for appropriate clichés.

"That guy over there," the man replied, "that's Pat. He's the GC. Go talk to him."

I made my way over, noting that Pat was the only one who wasn't sweating . . . or working, for that matter. He was dressed in pressed khakis and a golf shirt and was talking with a yummy mummy straight from the cast of *Desperate Housewives*. Logic said she was the homeowner. Her body language and facial gestures indicated irritation, while Pat's indicated, uh, the opposite of irritation. Bemusement? Eventually the woman left.

"Pat?" I said. "I'm here about the laborer's job."

He looked me over and deduced that laboring wasn't my normal gig.

"That's a job that involves a lot of work," he said. Several images flashed through my mind, including a twenty-five-mile forced march with a sixty-pound pack, as did the words "Today's training will enable you to break a man's windpipe using only your thumb."

"I need work," I said.

"You're hired," he said. "Follow me."

Twenty minutes later we pulled into the yard of a home in the country. The place looked half finished, but not the good kind of half finished: half finished like a guy intent on pulling an eight-day bender looks after day number four. Even to a construction neophyte, it smelled like a place where the owners either ran out of money or just ran.

"This is a remodeling project," Pat said to me through the rolled-down window of his truck. "I hate remodeling projects."

"Me too," I thought.

"You're gonna do the demolition," he said. "The tools you'll need are in the kitchen area. I've marked everything that comes out with red spray paint. Rip it out and drag it out to the Dumpster."

"Have you got a minute to walk me through it?"

"It ain't rocket science," Pat replied. "Leave the framing and the wiring in place, and tear out the sheetrock, doors, molding, and windows. The whole kitchen and both bathrooms go, too."

"Okay."

"It should take you about seven days. I'll check on you in three. Be here at eight, and leave at five."

"Okay."

"Any questions?"

Now, being a former white-collar guy who thinks things through, the answer to that question was, "Why, yes, you maniac, I do." After all, it's not too much to ask to have the little issues explained . . . issues like pay, mileage, lunch, insurance, maybe even some training on how to actually complete the job at hand. But, being a stranger in a strange land, I decided to go with the flow. "No questions."

With that, Pat pulled away.

I walked inside and, after checking out everything that was marked for removal, wondered why we weren't just using dynamite.

It occurred to me as I worked through the demo process over the next few days that the demolition of a home could certainly yield one of those cute little books people love with titles like *Everything I Needed to Know I Learned from Snuggling with My Mommy While Eating Vegetable Soup*. To internalize these concepts properly, you need a little suspension of disbelief. Just envision these words written in some curlicue font, listed one to a page, and illustrated by the guy who drew Winnie the Pooh. Okay, you ready? Get philosophical:

- *Try as you might, you cannot hurt an inanimate object.*

- *An inanimate object can, however, hurt you.*

- *It's always worth the effort to move the ladder.*

- *Righty, tighty. Lefty, loosey.*

- *Any satisfaction that comes from using a bigger hammer is negated by the toil required to clean up the mess.*

- *The human mind's greatest battle is the struggle between the desire for the right tool and the rationalization that it's not worth the energy to retrieve it.*

- *It's always worth the energy to get the right tool.*

- *The human brain cannot retain the above fact for more than six minutes.*

- *There is no problem so great it cannot be overcome with enough leverage.*

- *No amount of leverage can remove a screw.*

- *No amount of cussing can remove a screw.*

- *Working more than five days straight in the construction business cultivates an overwhelming desire to kick someone's ass.*

During my seven days as a demolition man, I made a point of checking the invoices presented by the Dumpster picker-upper guys, which indicated the weight of the load dropped off at the county landfill. In seven days, yours truly demolished and carried to the Dumpsters just shy of thirteen tons of material. And yet not a single muscle grew, and not even a hint of an ab appeared. How can you carry thirteen tons in seven days and not get at least a little buffing? All I got was sore.

A few interesting things about what homes are made of did, however, reveal themselves. Some factoids for your consideration:

a) Sheetrock has, arguably, the most perfect name in the English language. This is because it goes on in big *sheets*, and comes off as little teeny-tiny *rocks*.

b) Insulation, aka fiberglass, also has an appropriate name, because inside all that pink fluffy fiber are tiny shards of *glass*. If you take off your shirt and carry the fiberglass insulation to a Dumpster while holding it under your arms and over your shoulder, you can absorb enough of these shards into your skin to then clean yourself with Windex.

c) As children, the symbol of the carpenter we knew was the hammer. If you look into the construction of a new home, you will find it is now a nail gun. The nail gun should actually be named the nail machinegun, as carpenters use it the way Tony Montana used his in the final three minutes of *Scarface*.

d) If there were any justice in the world, the guy who invented PVC pipe would be worth $54 billion, and Bill Gates would be just another nerd working at Radio Shack.

Framers

The general contractor, Pat, told me to stay on-site and act as a runner and cleanup monkey after the demolition was done. He said I had potential in the business, because he'd lied about the demo timeline: he expected me to take at least two weeks and was shocked the job was complete in just over one. He paid me with four Benjamins, cash.

"Maybe having an actual worker on-site will inspire the subs to spend less time sitting in the shade," he said.

After he left, I promptly sat in the shade to await the arrival of the framing carpenters. In fact, I sat so long that my butt got sore, so I went home.

The framers were on-site when I got there in the morning. They had their compressors set up and were already firing their belt-fed nail guns on full automatic. It was quite a sight to see, as the walls of the new rooms took shape before my eyes in hours, not days.

House framers, in case you don't know, are the guys who build the bone structure for the home. They wear big tool belts that click-clack with all their gear when they walk, and they don't seem to say much. With the tool belts and the nail guns, they have a sort of cowboy thing going on, and cowboys don't talk much either. For a framer, a big on-the-job conversation is "Six foot, three and an eighth!" The response is the scream of a table saw producing said board. I pitched in by carrying the boards from the cutter to the nailer, and kept track of how many times "thank you" was utilized to express their appreciation. That would be zero times.

During lunch on their second day on the job, I dragged the cutter into a conversation by asking him how long he'd been a carpenter.

"I'm a framer," he said.

With that conversation clearly tapped out, I asked the other guy if he enjoyed being a framer.

"Sucks," he said.

Man, we were plum talked out.

When the framers did talk, it was for one reason: to rip apart the craftsmanship of the guy who'd gone before them. Apparently, this is a trait true of everyone in the building industry. If the framer before them did a perfect job, the criticism was about overkill. ("What kind of !#%* jerkwad doubles up his studs? Lookit this. What a freakin' waste.") If the guy before made the most minuscule of errors, the criticism was even more merciless. ("This wall is a one-sixteenth out of plumb . . . good God, I'll bet there ain't a straight angle in the whole #*$ structure. What a freakin' menace.") I listened very carefully for a kind word, but it wasn't forthcoming.

Because it was a renovation job, the framers completed their work in three days. After packing up their truck, the two of them stood and admired their handiwork. They seemed to be proud of their craft.

"Pretty amazing," I said. "It completely transforms the feel of the structure."

"Just gonna cover it with sheetrock," said the nailer.

"I hate renovation jobs," said the cutter.

Strangely, we haven't kept up.

Electricians

The next day, I sat on my butt waiting for the electricians.

The day after that, I sat on my butt waiting for the electricians. At four o'clock, Pat the contractor came by and asked me where the electricians were. I confessed that I wasn't fully in the loop regarding the subcontractor schedules.

On Thursday, the electricians arrived and stormed in as a pack of four, with an additional guy who was clearly the electrical boss man. Several minutes later, Pat and the homeowner arrived, and the entire entourage traipsed through the house as the homeowner described in detail what he wanted. Not a single note was taken.

After about thirty minutes, the homeowner left, with both Pat and the electrical boss swearing blood oaths to him that this was their top-priority job. Pat stood and conferred with the electrical boss until the homeowner was out of sight, then bolted himself. The electrical boss waited until Pat was out of sight, and he bolted. I wondered what jobs were their bottom priority.

Without so much as an additional detail from the bosses, the electricians began wiring the house for the new rooms. Since I'd never taken physics and passed physical science with a 69.5, the process appeared to be chaos. They hung their wires from a spool, then pulled the line out to the places it was supposed to go. To me, it looked like a linear Rubik's Cube. Among the things I didn't understand were: (a) Why didn't they just inspect the existing wire and leave it in place? (b) Why did they tear out the old wire before putting in the new wire, thus causing confusion about what wire went where? (c) Why does electrical wire smell so much like marijuana?

Unlike the framers, the electricians were talkers. They discussed steroids in baseball, Jeff Gordon's sexual orientation, the propensity of Nebraska to play a weak schedule, and whether "them terrorists need a nuke up their ass." Except for their keen insight and unanimous opinion concerning the deployment of nuclear arms, I'd never heard such a vast swing of opinions among friends. Jeff Gordon was a stud; Jeff Gordon was a twerp. Nebraska sucked; Nebraska ruled. Barry Bonds was a juiced-up A-hole cheater; Barry Bonds was — well, they all agreed on Barry Bonds. Rarely did their conversation stray from sports (and onto things electrical), except when one electrician asked if the others had seen the new Xbox release of a game called *Death by Claw Hammer.*

As the rookie, the thing that bothered me was that none of their talking ever drifted to the task at hand . . . which involved the most complex aspect of homebuilding. One slight mix-up by the electrician, and the homeowner is walking into the living room to turn on the kitchen lights. One slip of the X-Acto knife, and the homeowner wouldn't need to get out of bed to roast his marshmallows. It worried me. Finally I asked one of the electricians a question.

"How do y'all keep straight who's running what wire where?"

"It's hard," he said, "on these remodeling jobs."

"I hate remodeling jobs," I replied.

"I love 'em," the electrician replied. "If the house burns down, who's to say it was our wiring and not the previous builder's?"

On Monday morning the electricians didn't show up. Hindsight revealed that they were finished with the thing called "the rough-in," and now they had to wait for an inspection and sheetrocking before they finished their job. With no electricians around, there was nothing for me to do but clean the work site from top to bottom. That took about five hours, and then . . . I once again sat on my butt until quitting time. Note to self: keep a book in the car.

Tuesday — no one. It was, however, a nice day for reading in the shade. In all fairness, if this job offered some sort of potential career with advancement, perhaps there would have been some motivation to track down the contractor. But it didn't. So I didn't.

Wednesday — no one. Another book, but the heat was spiking. Fortunately, it was a cheap paperback, so the fact that my sweat poured onto the pages didn't bother me.

On Thursday, wisdom reared its beautiful head and generated with it a cooler of beer in the car. Modesty required that the beer remain untouched until noon so I wouldn't be, you know, an alcoholic, but I was half in the bag by five. The construction gig was shaping up nicely.

Friday came and, just prior to my first beer, Pat and the female half of the ownership rolled up. I stashed the cooler and set my course on intercept.

After sliding alongside them, it became clear they were well into an awkward silence. I spoke to break the tension.

"How's it going, boss man?"

"Where are the plumbers?" he asked accusingly. "They should already have their rough-in done. They said they were starting on Tuesday."

At this moment, several responses came to mind:

a) "Good question, boss. Unfortunately, I've been so busy with my reading and drinking I hadn't noticed."

b) "Hey, here's an idea: if you at least *drove by* every few days you wouldn't be so surprised about this kind of thing."

c) "Who cares? It's Friday. Anyone want a beer?"

"I don't know what's going on here," Pat told the still silent homeowner. "The plumbers and the HVAC guys were supposed to be ready for inspection today."

"Is this going to set back our timeline?" the woman asked. "We've got to be in in a month."

"No, no, no," Pat said. "We can make that . . . but I'm getting on the horn and chewing some ass today."

"You're sure we're okay with the timeline?" the woman asked.

"I'm sure," Pat replied.

The homeowner left. Pat stood there looking concerned until she was out of sight.

"Subs screwed you, huh?" I asked.

"Nah," he said, "I got 'em on another job."

Pat handed me $250 and turned to leave.

"My pay seems to be going down, boss."

"Want to tell me what you did this week?"

"Pay seems about right, boss," I said. "See you Monday."

HVAC Madmen

On Monday, the Marines of the construction world landed.

I bestow on them that compliment, because Marines are always assigned the hardest jobs in the worst conditions with the worst equipment. And those words describe the Heating/Ventilation/Air-Conditioning (HVAC) madmen in spades.

Out of respect for the pain and horror these men endure, let's discuss their ordeal in the format of a military order:

Situation: The perfectly good ductwork needs to be torn out of the residence located directly to our north.

Mission: Remove said ductwork before day's end.

Execution: Duct Team Alpha, wearing only blue jeans and heavy metal concert T-shirts, will advance on the position in a frontal assault. Upon arrival in the attic, Team Alpha will fan out to the flanks, ignoring the fact that the temperature in said attic has climbed from 97 degrees (F) to 140 degrees (F), with a heat index of 185. Team Alpha shall restrain themselves from the desire to blow their brains out.

Action: Team Alpha will commence to intertwine themselves with the attic's rafters, roof supports, and fiberglass insulation. Whenever possible, team members will rub their exposed skin against the insulation, absorbing shards of fiberglass until the skin to shard ratio is even. No less than once every minute, team members shall smash their exposed shins against the rafters, rip their skin on the nails protruding from the roof, and crush their exposed forearm bones against support beams. Use of foul language is authorized to alert other members of the team to your ongoing successes in these areas. All removed ductwork must be shoved through impossibly small breaks in the support beams, then collected later.

Command, Control, and Logistics: The commander of the operation will be as far away as possible in order to better ignore the pain his men will be in. He will bill the homeowner six times what he pays each worker. There will be water available in the van but unavailable to each team member during their actual work. The use of knee pads, elbow pads, shin pads, long-sleeved cotton shirts, water bottles, and safety glasses is authorized . . . but the criminally low wages paid to individual team members will discourage investment in these items. Any individual purchasing these items is to be called a wussy by other team members.

*   *   *

The HVAC lunatics executed the above order with a frightening intensity. In order to assist, I dragged the ductwork
out of the attic and out into the Dumpster . . . a fairly easy
job, but one that they immensely appreciated. Just as a stray
and beaten dog loves its new adoptive owner, these guys
loved me. This is because they'd never had anyone on a job
site even acknowledge them, much less assist them. When
they completed the removal task (in one-tenth of the time
you or I would have taken), they guzzled some water and
dove back in . . . to replace the ductwork they'd just torn
out with ductwork that looked exactly the same. It was a
Tasmanian Devilish event, and the air was filled with grunts,
groans, cusswords, and the rip of duct tape. It thrilled me to
see, for the first time in my life, duct tape being used for its
actual purpose. I pulled duct up into the attic for them, but
to say "I helped" would be like saying the guy who handed
Lance Armstrong his water bottles was the Tour de France
"co-winner."

    The next step occurred through some kind of HVAC
black magic. The situation is this: Have you ever looked
into your attic to see the huge tin box called the air handler?
(It's the inside version of that R2D2-looking thing that sits
outside.) If you have, you've no doubt wondered, "How in
the name of Hogan's Goat did they get that thing up
here?" It almost always sits in a place where the physical
laws of matter prevent it from being. It's the size of a big-
screen TV lying on its side, yet the opening into the attic is

the size of a dishwasher. One plus one does not equal 1.4, so it's a virtual impossibility that the air handler got where it got. Skeptics should go look at their air handler.

Anyway, the placement of the air handler was something I wanted to see. The guys broke for lunch, so I made a run to the store to pick up some Gatorade. Since the home under renovation was out in the country, the drive took fifteen minutes, and of course every minimum-wage worker in the county was in front of me in line investing in Lotto tickets, so the total trip took almost an hour. When I got back, the air handler was mysteriously in place . . . and yes, it was fitted behind a series of two-by-four supports that couldn't possibly allow for its placement. For you and me to get the thing in there, we'd have needed a crane and a roof removal team, but there it was, looking like it had been welded together on the spot. I wanted so bad to ask, but fear prevented me. What if it *was* black magic? As a God-fearing man, that knowledge needed to remain outside of my psyche.

For the next thirty minutes, the HVAC team connected the ducts to the air handler, then began packing their tools.

"Where are y'all going?"

"This is just the rough-in," they said. "We'll be back after the inspection."

Insert the sound of crickets.

"Ah, yes. The rough-in. Of course."

The Plumbers

The next morning, the plumbers arrived.

Your impression of a plumber is no doubt something akin to that guy Schneider on that old sitcom *One Day at a Time*. You know, a dude with a tool belt and a pipe wrench and some old blue jeans looking for an excuse to expose the butt crack they're supposed to hide.

That is not the case with construction plumbers. These guys rolled in like a platoon of combat engineers. They had a backhoe, a concrete cutter, a jackhammer, a water tank, six miles of water pipe, and a partridge in a pear tee.

"Okay," said the honcho. "What's the plan?"

I looked around to see who he was speaking to. He meant me.

"Dude, I'm the cleanup guy."

The honcho got on his Nextel walkie-talkie phone and called our mutual boss man, Pat. Then something unbelievable happened. Over the walkie-talkie, Pat gave the plumber the instructions. Now, I'm far from a perfectionist, but who would have ever thought that the detailed instructions for a master bathroom could be summed up as "Cut some concrete for the toilet, tub, and sinks, run it outside and stub it off, then trench down to the septic tank for tie-in. They'll need a pump, too, 'cause it's uphill."

Where are the tape measures? Where are the drawings? Where are the engineers and their slide rules? Where's the angst over what the homeowner actually wants?

The honcho looked over the bathroom for a full ten

seconds; then, using his finger to draw in the air, he said to his concrete guys, "Cut here; cut here; cut here." Then he walked out front.

Using equal precision, he pointed and said to the backhoe team, "Trench down that way, put the pump in about there, and tie in to the septic tank."

Returning inside, he said to his piping team, "Pressure-check the existing system, then run pipe to water the bathroom and the new half-bath."

"They have a sink going into the wet bar area," I offered.

"Really?" the honcho said. "Okay, water that too."

And with that, the honcho bolted.

For the next five hours, the plumbers destroyed the place. Between the banshee scream of the concrete cutter, the pounding of the jackhammer, the dust flying, the backhoe beeping its intention to reverse its course, and the piles of dirt collecting, it looked and sounded like Boston's Big Dig, but less organized. If the homeowners had walked in, they would have wept. At 2:00 p.m., the home looked beyond repair, short of bringing in a wrecking ball.

And then they reached the point of return.

For the next three hours, they filled in and covered up and cemented over and swept up, and at 5:00 p.m. . . . well, it didn't look like they'd ever been there. Sure, there was fresh dirt out front from the trenching, and there was a fine layer of concrete dust covering every inch of the house, but they'd somehow managed to take that war zone and repair it. Impressive. Then, of course, I realized that someone was going to have to clean up that fine layer of concrete dust.

It was time to go home and lie down.

Vacation Benefits

The next day I cleaned dust. All day. About 3:00 p.m., Pat rolled up.

"Okay," he said through his truck's window, "I won't need you for the next ten days."

"What gives?"

"Owners are going on vacation."

"So?"

"I ain't gonna put guys on a job where the owners aren't even in town."

"Aren't we going to miss the move-in deadline?"

Pat was still laughing as he rolled up the window.

Post-Vacation

Pat had me back on the work site the day the owners returned. I was inside removing tumbleweeds when they walked in, clearly excited to see all the work accomplished in their absence. It took about three minutes for them to realize what had occurred, and their faces grew long. In short order, they both looked like Mr. Ed.

Finally, the inevitable happened. The woman got mad.

"Exactly what in the hell have you been doing?" she asked me.

Good question. Please choose from the responses below:

a) "Vacationing."

c) "Wondering if a jury would convict you for killing me."

d) "No hablo Inglés."

All signs of courage and humor evaporated from my mind.

"I'm just a cleanup guy," I said.

"Well," she replied, "what work has been done that required you to clean up after it? I don't see a single thing. Not one #*&! thing."

"I think there've been some scheduling issues."

"Scheduling issues? We're supposed to be living here in ten days!"

"I realize, but — Hey! Look! It's Bigfoot! In the tree line!"

Just then, Pat rolled in. He got out of his truck and strutted up like he was delivering the keys and the certificate of occupancy.

"Morning," he said.

The woman went off. After five minutes of making points — all of which were true — she stopped. And glared.

Pat shook his head, indicating his rejection of everything she said. It was contractor language for, "I'm rubber, you're glue. Everything you say bounces off me and sticks to you."

"Look," he said. "We're lucky to be where we are. With all the changes you've made to the plans, you should be happy."

"Changes? What changes?"

"You've made lots of changes."

"What changes?"

"Like when you added those two windows. It threw off the schedule for an entire week."

"What other changes?

"There have been lots. I knew I should have started documenting them."

"This is insane."

"Plus, the inspector has held us up for seven days."

"Why?"

"I don't know. I called for the inspection, and he hasn't showed."

"Have you called him back?"

"Look, this isn't a big deal," Pat said. "We'll make the move-in date."

This defused the woman.

And I'll tell you why: most people have never conducted a business transaction where every single word the other guy says is a lie. As a result, they get tripped up by contractors. It would be like calling a family meeting, asking the kids if they want to go to Disney World or Hawaii for the family vacation, and the nine-year-old says, "I want to stay home and be a crack whore." There's no response, because it's too unreal . . . as is dealing with a contractor who lies every time his lips move.

"You really think we'll be in?" the woman said.

"Sure," Pat said. "Sheetrock one day. Mud and sand one day. Paint one day. Tie up the plumbing and install the fixtures, and we're done."

"That sounds doable," the woman replied.

As does traveling at the speed of light.

In Hell, Everyone Hangs Rock

The next morning, the advance team of the sheetrock crew showed up with the sheets of sheetrock. They unloaded them with a mini-crane and drove off without saying a word. I decided to make myself useful and began moving the sheets inside. What's the big deal, right? Move them one at a time, a total of no more than fifteen yards.

This turned out to be really, really hard work. Time to sit in the shade.

At one o'clock, five Mexicans rolled into the yard, each in his own car, all of which were nicer than mine. Their movement to action was something that would make even the most anal commando team leader jealous. There was no wasted time, movement, or chatter. They just filed over to the vast mound of sheetrock that had been delivered and began snapping them up — two and three at a time — and carrying them into the house with an ease I can barely manage carrying a six-pack.

After positioning the sheetrock in the various staging areas, they went straight to work, without so much as a "Here's the plan." It's hard to describe how they do it, because you have no point of reference. Imagine getting your family packed for a cross-country move without anyone speaking. Anyway, the general gist is this: One guy sets up to cut the sheetrock. Two guys put on these miniature stilts and arm themselves with cordless drills to "hang the rock" floor to ceiling. One guy gets a measuring tape and begins measuring the areas to be covered by the rock.

And one guy sets up to sand the rock's rough, post-cut edges.

Then the machine starts. In a fluid blur of human synchronicity, they all go into motion and the air fills with the horror known as sheetrock dust. The measuring guy gives the cutter the specs, the cutter cuts, the sander sands, the measuring guy grabs the piece, slaps it against the wall, and the stilt guys screw it in. Almost instantly, their jobs begin to meld, and the crew is delivering to the stilt guys sheets of rock as fast as they can be screwed in. And that's really, really freakin' fast. It is an absolute certainty that they could hang four sheets of rock faster than you and I could agree on the measurements of the first piece.

Within five hours, at least half the house was sheetrocked, and the work site looked like a training camp for suicide bombers. There were pieces of rock scattered everywhere, the dust was a quarter inch thick, and sheetrock mud was splattered across the floor. Why did the area look so bad? Because not only had the Mexicans not stopped to clean up, they hadn't stopped. No water breaks, no rest breaks, no pull the underwear out of their crack breaks . . . nada. Just one continuous blur of motion, with hardly a drop of sweat to show for it.

Since it was now six o'clock, an hour past my quitting time, I bolted. Surely they'd follow soon.

The next morning, the house was done.

Done.

They'd rocked everything, slapped on the first layer of mud in the cracks, wrapped the doorways . . . It was unbelievable. If I had stayed to watch and fallen asleep, they would have surely sheetrocked me.

There is something you need to know about this phase of construction if you ever plan to build or renovate your house, which is this: you shouldn't witness it. It is impossible for a nonprofessional construction person to see this residential apocalypse and envision it one day being a home. It is the Martha Stewart equivalent of opening the oven and seeing a wharf rat eating the soufflé. The floor is four inches deep in dust and pieces of sheetrock. The wires are hanging out of the future receptacles. The cracks are covered with miscolored, unsanded mud. There is no molding, no trim, no kitchen, no fixtures. It is as ugly a scene as a future homeowner could see. Oh, and that's what the lady of the house saw when she walked in right behind me.

As the mess was technically hers, her lip quivered. As the guy who had to clean it up, my lip quivered. Together, we hated Pat. If neither of us had been married, the moment would have bonded us as soulmates.

Tile Is Two Pieces

After a full day of cleaning up after the sheetrockers, I arrived to find Pat at the work site, looking around like a geologist who's discovered a new cave. It's hard to describe, but he had a look that somehow said, "Wow, this is kind of cool. I wonder how all this happened."

When he realized there was another person in the room, he advanced to one of the socket holes and inspected it as if — with great care — he was checking for its quality. Right. It's quite possible that thirteen-year-old boys care more about a centerfold's "ambitions" than Pat cared about what his subcontractors were doing.

"Hey, I need you to rip out the tile in both bathrooms," he said. "The tile guys are coming tomorrow."

Knowing there would be no further guidance, I gathered my tools and set out for the bathroom. Here is a brief list of things that don't remove floor tile: violent swings of a sledgehammer. Sidearm swings of a clawhammer. Foul language.

No, friend, there's only one way to remove floor tile: a chisel, a hammer, and fifty thousand tap-tap-taps.

Tap-tap-tap, pop . . . the piece of tile pops loose. Tap-tap-tap, crack-pop . . . the tile breaks in half, and half pops loose. Repeat. For seven hours.

The next day, after spending seven hours going tap-tap-tap, crack-pop, it is important to be on the scene when the tile guys arrive. It is important because you don't want to miss it when they walk into the bathroom, and say, "Who was the freakin' idiot who pulled up the individual tiles?" You don't want to miss this, because you need to be able to say, "What's wrong with that?"

This is when the tile guys say, "Because tile is glued to big-ass pieces of backer board. You don't remove each tile . . . you pull up the backer board. Pull up maybe four or five pieces of backer board and you're done. Tile comes with it."

Hell hath no fury like a woman scorned? My ass.

Go to Trim School, Young Man

The next craftsman to enter my world was the trim carpenter. He rolled up in what was arguably the most dilapidated vehicle I'd seen since my lost weekend in Tijuana in 1989. He wiggled his girth out of the truck, set up his cutting tools, and promptly got to the business of sweating.

I watched as he prepared to "trim out" the first room, and it was impossible not to feel sorry for him. His glasses were crooked, his T-shirt was full of holes, his jeans were Wal-Mart via Goodwill, and he had only a stubby pencil for writing down his measurements — which he did on a scrap piece of wood. I assumed that trim carpenters must be on the bottom of the food chain, and that he was making only a little dough more than me.

Then . . . *artistry* began to emerge from this unlikely figure. He swirled with motion, pulling trim, chopping, dropping, pulling, chopping, and dropping. Over the next hour, a pile of sticks of various shapes and sizes would grow beside him, and just as suddenly as he started he would stop. He'd then gather the sticks, move into the room he'd measured, and the nail gun would start: bam, bam, bam, bam, bam, bam, bam. The pile of sticks would transform themselves into trim, each piece fitting into place with the exactness of a physics formula. Crown molding, floorboards, door trim, window trim . . . bam, bam, bam, bam, bam. An hour later, he would emerge, the room fully trimmed. And by God that room was *transformed* . . . from a lip-quivering, hopeless mess of collateral damage to looking like a room in the making.

For the next three days, I cleaned up after the trim carpenter. His work ethic was frightening: maybe a sip of water between finishing rooms, and a baloney sandwich on white bread for lunch while standing at his chop saw. Never before has an hourly employee worked with such intensity. I wondered if he had nine children at home and his drive to feed them provided his endless energy. When he was done, a miracle had occurred. The house was breaking free from its cocoon, and a home was beginning to emerge. The owner's wife arrived at the end of day three as the trim carpenter was packing his equipment, and she *ran* from room to room. She shrieked. Twice.

"Hey, man," I said. "The place looks awesome."

"Thanks," he said, attempting for the thousandth time that day to keep his glasses from falling off.

"If you don't mind my asking, is the money in trim decent? I mean, how much did you get paid for this job?"

"Well," he said, "I've still got to do the mantel and the fireplace, and that's a separate price . . . but for what I've done so far it was $3,500."

Aaaaaand . . . cut!

Where are the hidden cameras?

"Three thousand five hundred dollars?"

"Yeah."

"That's a three and a five, followed by two zeroes?"

"Yup."

"Dude, that puts you way north of $100 an hour."

"I guess," he said.

"Dude, you make as much as a lawyer."

"True. But I do something productive."

And away he drove, leaving behind a laborer filled with awe, and a new answer to the hypothetical question, "If you could go back in time and learn a different profession, what would it be?"

ABC Construction . . . We Actually Show Up!

On Friday of that week the construction gig ended. Three months of work on one house, and I'd seen all there was to see. Pat came by in the afternoon and peeled off three Benjamins, then told me that on Monday he was moving me to a new site. Just for fun, I told him one of the subs had hired me away, and the circle was complete.

I learned a lot about the building business, but most of it is stuff a regular human simply doesn't want to know. This pains me, because several of my friends are extremely reputable, successful home builders and are nothing like Pat "the builder." They sweat the details, kill themselves to be prompt and courteous, and are willing to lose some money if they make a mistake. Methinks, however, that they aren't the norm.

Perhaps now is a good time to give you a succinct explanation of the world of contracting, in case you ever decide to build, remodel, or hire anyone to do anything more than change a light bulb. Here goes:

The general contractor is the guy that you hire to hire the people who actually do the work on your project. When you give him money, he will use it to pay the guys who finished up his *last* project. In order for him to have money to pay the people on your project, he will need a new project and will use the money from the new project to pay the guys on your project, which is the same economics used by drug dealers in the projects.

Subcontractors are modern-day serfs, as they are tied to the general contractor the way serfs were tied to the land. This because the general contractor owes them money for so many projects that they have lost count, and to leave the contractor means to leave uncollected money on the table. How much, they aren't sure . . . but they assume that the general contractor, because he has a nice truck, is keeping tabs on the past projects. At some point during your project, the general contractor will give the subcontractors money from somewhere, and the circle continues. No one really knows who is owed what, but as long as payroll is met, the circle can continue. Philosophically, it appears the industry is an endurance contest — which starts and stops each time a general contractor declares bankruptcy. Strangely, this is always a surprise . . . and the money owed to the subs gets officially erased. Of course, the contractor reincorporates in a week with a new name, and — wink-wink — assures the subs that he'll make it up to them. The result is like a drug-laden, spouse-hitting, bean-dipping, Pabst-drinking, trailer-park marriage.

Sadly, this Jerry Springer life in a tool belt *does* apply to you.

Why? A few reasons.

1) Consider this: you must pay a contractor in order for him to pay the subcontractor, who must pay the supplier in order to get more materials in order to keep working for the contractor. If you look closely, you see that nowhere in this priority list is payment of the guys who work *for* the subcontractor and ultimately do that little thing called the work. With the work taking such a low priority, the guys who do the work are always on the lookout for another boss who might have the money to actually pay them. So it's very possible that you could pay the contractor, who will use *your* money to pay the subcontractor on *another* project, which results in *your* workers leaving *your* project to work for a subcontractor on another project, in order to be paid with *your* money.

2) Every now and then, too much money ends up floating, and everyone gets nervous. So if, say, your contractor has a vacation planned and doesn't have two *future* projects under way to feed him money so he can pay the subcontractor, and the subcontractor is feeling neglected, the sub can take action. How? He simply goes to the courthouse and proclaims you owe him money . . . even though you've never laid eyes on him or his crew, never agreed to hire them, there's nothing in writing, and you've paid the contractor twice what he originally estimated. The court says, "Oh, you poor, hardworking, salt-of-the-earth, trustworthy man! Here, let's put a mechanic's lien on that bastard's house." This kind of lien is very nice for the subcontractor, because no one notifies *you* about it and there's no recourse to it. It is his own little sleeper-cell 401(k),

which remains dormant until . . . until . . . you go to sell the house! Then, ta-dah! You get to pay the guy for the work you paid the contractor for a decade ago! And the system is seamlessly perfect, because if you go after the contractor, he's four bankrupt corporations removed from the one he owned when he worked for you.

3) Once you have been with a contractor long enough for him to do the demo, or build the foundation, you are his. Why? Because once one of those things is done, no other contractor wants the job. And if you fire your contractor, you can't get any subs to work for you, because they are all working for contractors hoping to get paid for their previous project.

And for these reasons, my plans are under way to start a contracting franchise business. Think I'm kidding? Here's the concept . . . which will sound like absolute brilliance to any reader who has ever dealt with a contractor:

Name: ABC Construction
Motto: We actually show up!

(*Ring, ring*) "Hello, ABC Construction . . . Uh, no ma'am, we don't bid jobs. But when you get all those bids, feel free to add thirty percent to the highest bid, then call back to hire us. Why? *Because we actually show up.* Oh, you think that's NOT a big deal? This is your first construction project, isn't it? Okay . . . Well, when you fire your contractor, please call us. Of course, that will qualify as a rescue job, so you'll need to add forty percent to the project cost and we'll finish it for you."

(Ring, ring) "ABC Construction . . . You got our name from a friend? You've built a home before? Yes, it's true . . . we do offer a special program where we only work on your home and don't have forty-two other projects going, but it costs an additional two hundred percent. Stop crying, ma'am. Yes, I realize you're happy . . . Let's see, we can book you in for 2013. Does that work for you?"

(Ring, ring) "ABC Construction . . . Oh, hello, Mrs. Cleaver. What? We made a mistake and built the door in the wrong spot? Okay, would you like us to be passive-aggressive and surly and aloof and pretend it's your fault? Or would you like our Changes with a Smile program where we just charge an additional thirty-five hundred dollars and do the work without all the mind games? One Smile program coming up . . . We'll have a man out there today. Stop crying, Mrs. Cleaver. Yes, I realize you're happy."

So, should you toss it all and become a construction laborer? As a minion at the bottom of the food chain, it was certainly better than scooping ice cream or delivering pizza. The industry is for people who have a problem with authority. After all, there's virtually no adult supervision, and half the time your pay comes as cash. It is an industry for people who have a high threshold for physical pain and a low threshold for mental stimulation. There's a niche for everyone, from guys who like the idea of pulling electrical wire and risking their lives to guys who like filling Dumpsters and drinking beer before noon.

Will it be a good fit for you? Sure, assuming the local pirate ships aren't hiring and you can't afford the air fare to France to join the Foreign Legion. As for me, it was time for some air-conditioning.

Good Things Come in Big Boxes

When your average white-collar person thinks of the job from hell, there are the Big Two that come to mind: flipping burgers in a fast-food joint and working as an "associate" at a big-box store. To the white-collar mind, these two represent the end of the line — where life has simply beaten out of you any entrepreneurial thoughts or dreams, and even your attempts to mow lawns and sell crap on eBay have been augered into the ground like a wingless F-16. Are the Big Two as bad as you think? Let's find out. First, the big-box experience.

The history of the big-box store is an interesting one, and it's not very well known. In fact, Google provided zero hits on the subject. With no actual facts available, I contacted a writer for Wikipedia, and here is what he told me:

In the late 1960s, a man by the name of Vito "Hammerhead" Scarafile was convicted in New York for seven counts of racketeering, four counts of murder, and 285 counts of environmental contamination. When Vito agreed to flip on the Gallegio family, he was moved into the Witness Protection Program, given one million dollars, and assigned the name of Timothy Brady. He was relocated to a small town in southern Nebraska and told to stay out of trouble.

It took Tim only a few weeks to get a solid protection racket going down there in south Nebraska, and not long after that he had a decent loan-sharking gig going as well. The money-loaning scheme did so well, in fact, that Tim let his collections for protection fall behind. He figured, incorrectly, that his clients would proactively deliver the money, seeing how well protected they were.

As one might guess, Tim had a problem with his temper, which helps explain his anger upon discovering that both Winkler's Tractor Supplies and their Main Street neighbor Christian Pharmacy were two weeks behind. Tim did what he felt his professional ethics demanded, which entailed beating old man Winkler with a tire iron, then throwing him through the wall into Christian Pharmacy.

"Fix him up," Tim told Willie Shermer, the pharmacist. He watched as Willie scrambled for bandages, antiseptic, and pain meds.

"Hey," Tim Brady thought, "that's pretty frickin' convenient. I threw the old geezer right into a pharmacy."

Then, as if having one thought wasn't enough, he had another.

"You know," he pondered, "these pathetic hayseed hicks buy drugs, *and* they buy tractors. Maybe if I leave the hole in the wall, they'll buy a tractor while they wait for Willie to fill their prescriptions." Tim was so excited about the idea, he went to the edge of town and shot a pony to calm his nerves.

Tim's hunch was right. Tractor sales went up eight percent. It was then his crowning concept began to unfold.

Over the next eight months, Tim bribed the mayor, the town council, and all but one of the folks on the zoning board. The holdout on the zoning board had a wood chipper accident, and the groundwork was done. Next, Tim killed the local Redi-Mix cement dealer and married his wife. As a honeymoon present, he presented her with six acres of newly paved now-not-wetlands on the edge of town.

Next, Tim shut down the city's construction industry by hiring all the available craftsmen to build him a massive warehouse. His design instructions were fairly straightforward: "Make it, you know, like a big frickin' box. Nuttin' fancy. No fruity stuff." As the construction progressed, Tim went around to every retailer in town and carefully inventoried their goods. And he asked politely for the names of their suppliers and somehow got them every time.

From there, it was just some phone calls:

"Uh, yeah . . . Knitting World? Yeah, my name is Timmy Brady. Listen, der's dis store in my town, the Bumble Bee . . . How much yarn does dat old bat order from you each year? Dat right? I tell you what — why don't I buy *ten times* that from you, and we set up an exclusive relationship, huh? You like dat, doncha?"

It was an exciting day when Tim's big-box store opened. Named TiMart, it bore a slogan Tim had come up with himself: *"Stuff? I got your stuff right here."*

The following month, Tim attended an entrepreneur's seminar in Little Rock, Arkansas, billed as "The Power of the Idea!" He was feeling understandably proud of *his* idea and wanted to find out if he "could freakin' franchise it, or somethin'."

The first night of the conference, Tim met a man named Sam at the hotel's poolside tiki bar. He remembered him clearly, because his last name — Walton — stood out so vividly. In fact, he remembered after a few drinks asking Sam "if he had a wussy son named John Boy."

Sam, it seems, was particularly interested in Tim's concept, and kept him up late, moving the conversation to a gentleman's club named the Moisture Factory and buying rounds of expensive tequila and lap dances while pressing for detailed information concerning sales, gross profits, and the bottom-line "net net." The last thing Tim remembered was saying, "Sam, who freakin' cares about the details, ya business geek? You apply enough muscle, and the sheep get in line."

The next day at the conference, Tim couldn't find a trace of his new friend Sam, even at the Happy Hour free buffet. He assumed that Sam had hooked up with one of the dancers and was soaked in sweat at one of the airport motels surrounding the Little Rock airport. He smiled, thinking of his new friend's good fortune.

Three months later, Tim experienced an attack of such ugly violence that none of his years on the mean streets had prepared him for it: he'd killed men with his bare hands, with baseball bats, wire garrotes, machetes, even ice picks, but this new assault was the most horrific by far . . . from corporate lawyers. Within twenty-four hours, he was unable to open the front door of his mansion, because of the stacks of cease-and-desist orders and subpoenas and crates of discovery materials sent by the attorneys of his new "friend" Sam. Private investigators, photographers, and plaintiff's attorney video teams filled the streets, and Tim found it impossible even to talk on the phone due to all the static caused by the bugging. Sam, it seemed, had decided to steal Tim's idea and was carrying out a sneak attack with the most ruthless, amoral muscle known to man.

The details of what transpired over the next two weeks are sketchy, but rumors in the legal community are that Tim Brady was served with over 175 lawsuits in sixteen days by twenty-six different law firms. The final straw apparently occurred when a semi-famous bounty hunter kicked in his front door and punched Tim in the face as a preemptive strategy. Fists quickly gave way to cold steel, then to hot lead. When the police arrived, they declared that it was the first white-collar gunfight they'd ever encountered, but due to the layers of legal representation, it was impossible to tie anyone to anything. In the end, the bounty hunter walked and was put on retainer by nine of the law firms involved.

Although Tim, and ultimately his groundbreaking store called TiMart, died, his idea didn't . . . and from its ashes rose a phoenix, led by the family Walton. No, he didn't personally live to see the big-box store spread across the fruited plain, but don't mourn for Tim: it all worked out exactly as he envisioned it.

Love them or hate them, big-box stores are now an ingrained part of Americana. From sea to shining sea, they sell crap for less and as a result have wiped out thousands of mom-and-pop stores. In many cases, entire small towns have seen their entire Main Street economy snuffed out by these titans of trade. This makes it easy to feel self-righteous when discussing the damage these stores do.

The truth, however, is that the arguments against the big-box stores are a slippery slope and usually fraught with painful hypocrisy. Mom and Pop's work boots store would be doing just fine, thank you, except for the fact that while Mom's running the store, Pop is down at the big box himself. How can he pass up those low, low prices on Double Whammy bass lures? A pack of twelve is a buck and a half cheaper than at Skeeter's Bait Shop! And Skeeter would understand, right? Sure he would. Because Skeeter now buys his work boots at the big box. And the noose tightens.

The granddaddy of all big-box stores is, of course, Wal-Mart. Their statistics boggle the mind. In 2006 alone they sold more than $315 billion worth of junk and pocketed more than $11 billion in profits. There are only twenty-one nations with a gross national product greater than Wal-Mart's sales. Sam Walton's widow and kids? They are the low-price leaders to the tune of $80 billion in personal wealth. In case you are bad at math, the Walton family has more dough than the Gates and the Buffett families combined. Somebody somewhere is sweatshoppin' to the oldies, because you sure don't gather that sort of coin paying American union workers to go on break.

Over 127 million Wal-Mart haters shop there each week in the good old USA. In 2005, Wal-Mart gave away $245 million in cash to local American charities. And 1.3 million

Americans slip on their "How Can I Help You" vests each day, which makes Wal-Mart the biggest private employer in the land. (The federal government remains unimpressed; they have that many people call in sick each day.)

Is Wal-Mart good? Bad? That's for you to decide. But there is certainly one aspect to Wal-Mart's numbers that is scary: the statistics I quoted above are for *one* big-box chain. Imagine what they'd be if you added in Kmart, Target, Costco, Home Depot, Lowe's, Best Buy, Toys "R" Us, Barnes and Noble, Circuit City, Staples, and Office Depot. Friend, you can take the good old days of mom-and-pops and slip them right down the memory tube, because they are gone, and they aren't coming back.

In order to do my part within the assimilation process, today I applied to work for one of the big boxes: let's call it MegaMart. Applying is, in reality, a *vastly* different experience than what you would expect. You probably envision just going into the store, going to Customer Service, and having the lady look you over and say, "Pulse? Check. Vertical? Check. Here's your greeter vest."

Hardly.

No, applying for a job at MegaMart is only a little less nerve-racking than trying to get a job with the National Security Agency.

Here's why: *there is no human contact.*

How can that be? It's true. No human being discussed my potential employment with me, so there were no opportunities to say, "Yes, sir. No, sir." There was no way for them to know my pants weren't around my knees, or that I didn't have track marks on my arms, or tattoos on my face, or half a sewing kit stuck through my tongue. There was no way for me to, well, you know, *bull*——*t* my way through the door.

Instead, there was Little Brother.

Little Brother sat there like R2D2, glaring at me with his Press to Start screen saver glowing. He looked like one of those Wang Computer monstrosities from computer lab in the late '70s.

With bold defiance, I sat down and fingered the keyboard. This was no ordinary keyboard, however. After the Apocalypse, it will be the roaches and this keyboard. This was one seriously titanium-encased, rubber-keyed, lubricated-by-syrup, smash-and-spill-resistant keyboard. A *horse* could type on this thing, and . . . okay, enough about the keyboard.

The application process started strangely, by making me press "I agree" to about nine pages of legal disclaimers that would take an attorney $3,800 in billable hours to decipher. I agreed to everything, page after page after page, and probably gave the MegaMart board my 401(k). Who knows? Next, Little Brother asked my name, address, SSN, the usual stuff. Then it demanded my employment history, along with my work supervisors. It got stumped on this one under my Marines employment history, and wouldn't let me advance without a supervisor's name. Finally, I entered **First Name:** "President" and **Last Name:** "Bush, Sr." and it let me advance. Next, it asked if I wanted the application linked to every MegaMart within fifty miles. *And then* . . . it asked me to verify the information I'd given thus far, because I wouldn't be able to make changes after this point.

Whatever. Verified.

Then . . . Wait a minute. No changes? What the . . . Why make changes? Unless . . . unless there's some real heavy stuff coming down the pipe — stuff I might mess up on. And that's when it occurred to me: my application is getting logged into some sort of MegaMart Motherboard, and all it would take was a few stupid answers for me to be barred from MegaMarts everywhere.

My hands got a little sweaty as I hit Next.

And so began my sixty-four-question quiz.

The quiz started easy, basically Ethics for Felons. You choose from "Strongly Disagree," "Slightly Disagree," "Agree," and "Strongly Agree." The choices were things like:

- It's okay to steal from work.
- If I'm having a bad day, it would be okay to leave without permission.
- Quality isn't that important.

At this point, I'm sailing along.

- My friends would say I'm difficult to get along with.
- If I have a puppy and it goes doo-doo on the rug, I should smash it flat with a sledgehammer.

It felt good, kicking the profile booty. But then, the multiple choice:

Your supervisor advises you of new procedures concerning your workstation. You should: (a) Implement the new procedures. (b) Learn as much as possible about the new procedures. (c) Analyze the new procedures and consider how they will affect your time management. (d) Discuss with your supervisor your ideas for implementing the new procedures.

Hello? I want to work at MegaMart, not get a master's in management theory.

Next . . . You see a coworker violating a safety procedure repeatedly. You should: (a) Discuss with him the importance of safety. (b) Point the issue out to your supervisor so she can deal with it. (c) Mention to your coworker your concern about their safety. (d) Ask the coworker if you can assist, then set a good example by following the procedure correctly.

(Note to the Human Resources team at MegaMart: These aren't the kinds of questions that we the people can answer. In order to clarify what we can answer, let me provide you an example of what you should be asking. Here you go: Your supervisor calls in sick. In her absence, you should: (a) Work extra hard and strive for quality. (b) Use the opportunity to have a meth-snorting contest with the guys in shipping. (c) Stuff your underwear with merchandise, then quit at the end of your shift. (d) See if you can go the entire shift without making eye contact with a customer.

The test went on and on and on. For thirty minutes the torture continued, and all the while I was pondering the intent of the questions on a MegaMart application. What do they want to hear? What if the test is designed to catch people saying what they want to hear? What if they *like* the idea that you're trying to say what they want to hear? What did that 103-year-old greeter say to get hired? What did that cashier with the shaved eyebrows say?

Finally, mercifully, it was over. And Little Brother told me they'd call if they were interested.

The next day, the phone did not ring. Mr. White-collar, Auburn alum, BA in English, former Marine officer, award-winning creative director's phone did not ring. Ring it did not. I would've known if it rang, and let me assure you, there was no ringing happening on that particular phone. Its lack of ringing was, in fact, its most noticeable feature.

Three days. No call. I would've felt worse if my wife had laughed at me the first time she saw me in my altogether, but not a lot worse.

Today, big box #2 . . . Let's call it LumbeRus.

I assumed, correctly, that their hiring practices would be the same as MegaMart's, because in reality they are the same store selling different stuff. As a result, a quick search on the Internet put me face-to-face with their electronic application. I drilled down to find the store near me, then clicked on the spot that indicated Parking Lot Attendant. Being outdoors looked good — you know, wrangling carts, cleaning up broken glass . . . it sounded sort of cowboyish. Plus, there would be a minimum of supervision.

The application proceeded as expected, until I reached the dreaded LumbeRus Personnel Profile.

The first thing that came up was a basic bar chart indicating that September was the biggest month for LumbeRus in both sales and installations. Damn. This was going to be a freakin' economics question, or even worse, math. They were going to ask me what percentage decrease there was between September and December or to work a formula based on some seasonal economics theory and cyclical market forces. Then, to my complete surprise, they asked me what month the chart indicated was the biggest month for LumbeRus sales and installations.

Bring it on, lads.

Next section, the Agree or Disagree thing. This one was pretty easy (*I lose my temper if I don't get my way*), but they did have a few tricksters in there: *My friends don't refuse to not say that I'm not easily swayed to do the wrong thing when the right thing is not an option.* If it's a short-answer response, you could write, "The right thing to do is always the right thing to do. And the right thing to do here is to smash the guy who wrote that question in the teeth with a LumbeRus two-by-four." But as to agree/disagree? You tell me.

Or perhaps this little gem: *I need to carefully study an issue before I decide what to do.*

All right, dammit, let's work that one out:

MANAGER: Hey, Lowe. Go get the shopping cart that that Hummer just ran over and bring it here.
ME: I'm on it, boss. No study needed.

Or:

MANAGER: Hey, Lowe. There's a mercury-trigger anthrax bomb with redundant failsafe security measures under Register Six. Go defuse it.
ME: I'm on it, boss. I think it would be best for the corporation, however, if I spend a couple minutes studying protocols on www.defusing-for-dummies.com.

What the hell do these people want? As a leader in the Marines, you don't want your boys studying nuclear proliferation issues — their job is to stick their bayonets into bad guys. As a white-collar manager, you're damn right you want your people studying their options. What does LumbeRus want from a lot attendant? You got me. I couldn't even pass the stupid MegaMart test.

The ethics test, however, was mostly straightforward and fairly easy. Then, out of the blue, came this: *Alphabetize the following* —

Wait . . . will there really be stuff for me alphabetize if I scroll down? No way . . . Alphabetizing was what we did in third grade. Second grade, maybe. I scrolled down. It's alphabetizing for Mensa members:

12345abc
1234bca

a123bc4
a1b2c3d

Hmm, let's see. I choose 1*ki*2*ss*3*my*4*as*5*s*

Maraanne Aardvark
Mara Aardvark
Meera Aardvark
Maaria Aardvark
Aaaaaand, gun please.

There I am, Mr. White Collar, once again sweating out a test to be a damn parking lot attendant. No wonder the poor are so pissed off — they're smarter than you and me, and they still get tortured trying to get a job that won't pay the bills.

Finally, the test ended and was subsequently launched into cyberspace. And as I mashed that Enter button, a solemn vow was made to my ego: I *will* be working for LumbeRus, or I *will* be going *big-box* with my AR-15 and 1,000 rounds of ammo.

It's been a week, and every day I grow weaker. Ego deflating . . . testosterone decreasing . . . Are you with me here? Do you understand the ramifications? Zero calls from two out of two big-box stores.

Time for Plan B.

10 ccs of Sanity, Stat . . .

Okay, I failed to make Team Big-Box. Time to counter with Plan B: going after something with an intellectual challenge. Or at least as much intellectual challenge as can be achieved at near-minimum wage. Next stop, medicine.

Sure, now you're thinking, "What aspect of medicine requires little medical education and almost no additional training?" Well, there is one. But more on that later. First, let's find out what history has to say about medicine.

The earliest of early medicine, per se, began in the Neolithic period, also known as the New Stone Age. Yup, the Stone Age. This is not a time noted for intellectual achievement, as the finest of tools were made from, well, stone. So what were they doing that qualified as medicine? You're probably thinking archaeologists have found evidence of set bones or pulled teeth . . . something that a grunting, drooling, IQ-of-an-Irish-setter Stone Age dude could accomplish just out of sheer common sense. You would be wrong.

No, curious one, it is not something simple . . . not

stitches, or herbs, or crutches . . . your early ancestors were drilling holes in each other's skulls. Why? Who knows? Surely it seemed like a good idea at the time, what with all the anesthesia, antibiotics, and follow-up care available to a Neanderthal staggering around with his brains exposed to the elements.

Okay, fast-forward a few millennia: the first big name in Western medicine was Hippocrates. I use the word "Western" in the description because the Chinese had practically invented cholesterol screening before Western man came to the conclusion that, uh, drilling holes in each other's heads was a poor idea. Anyway, Hippocrates believed that the body's health revolved around four humors: yellow bile, black bile, phlegm, and blood. As you can see, Hippocrates receives perhaps more credit than he should, given that his theory ranks up there with rain dancing for practicality . . . although being three-fourths bile and phlegm may well apply to some of our esteemed senators in Washington. Anyway, Hippocrates did create the idea of a physician-patient relationship, where the physician puts the patient's well-being above all else. This was a big advance, and prohibited the physician from, say, drilling a hole in a patient's head because he was curious about what the patient was thinking.

For the next couple thousand years, medicine muddled forward like a bill in Congress. There was lots of bloodletting, and herbal potions, and leeches, and some really grim attempts at surgery, but mostly it was about patients needing help, then patients screaming in pain, then patients dying, then physicians getting together for a witch burning and drinks on Wednesday afternoons.

Eventually, the Renaissance and the Enlightenment arrived in Europe, and physicians began to figure things out . . . mostly by dissecting their dead patients. It was during this time that they figured out that blood circulates around the body, and that things called diseases exist, and that cures like "Swing a dead cat around your head six times, then bury it under an oak tree" don't actually work. In reality, not a lot of medicine got accomplished during this time, but there *was* some serious third grade biology being unearthed. Hey, you gotta start somewhere.

In the 1800s, medicine began to get some traction. In 1847, Ignaz Semmelweis made a breakthrough when working with women giving birth, which apparently went something like this:

SEMMELWEIS: Achtung, man! Your voman is giving birth! Come and help me!

FATHER: I am here, Doktor! What can I do to help?

SEMMELWEIS: What is that crap all over your hands?

FATHER: It is crap, Herr Doktor. I have been cleaning out the hog pen.

SEMMELWEIS: What if I need you to scratch my nose, Dummkopf! Go wash your hands!

And then . . . the woman *actually didn't die,* which must mean that death was a pretty frequent occurrence among Semmelweis's patients for him to notice this out-of-the-ordinary outcome. And thus word spread among physicians: if you wash your hands before sticking them inside someone, the patient is less apt to die.

With this stunning development out in the open, Western medicine staggered forward and eventually reached the point where it was saving more people than it was killing. Physicians became popular and began to make a very good living indeed. When insurance companies began noticing that the doctors were insuring bigger houses, they realized someone was making money without paying them protection. This was a serious problem, and the insurance companies dealt with it the way a loan shark deals with a crackhead who's short on this week's vig.

Before long, the insurance companies had the doctors paying malpractice insurance, disability insurance, employee liability insurance, building and equipment insurance, and key-man insurance. Somehow, the doctors managed to keep their practices open and still make a profit, so the insurance companies cut to the chase: they sold insurance to the doctors' patients, collected all the available money, then returned to the doctors exactly enough money to pay their insurance.

With all the physicians' wealth successfully transferred into the hands of the insurance companies, Western medicine entered its next phase of development, which historians are now calling the Collapse of the System phase. And where does this put you? Good question . . . I guess swinging a cat around your head six times and burying it under an oak tree.

Landing My Next Gig

I have a good friend who is an emergency medicine doctor; he was one of the guys who immediately recognized the lunacy of me quitting my job and reminded me of this fact whenever we went out to lunch and I pretended my wallet was at home. I called him up.

"Doc? Time for a different job."

"Well," he responded, "there's about thirty-five acres at the country place that needs cuttin' back and cleanup. That should take at least a couple months."

"Nope," I explained, "just got through doing the manual labor thing. It's time to work in the ER."

"Excellent," he said. "We've been discussing how badly we need an advertising guy on the floor. You could, you know, do brochures for the patients on chainsaw safety, and why it's so unhealthy to absorb 9mm bullets into their thoracic cavity."

"Funny. I'm talking about working on the floor."

"Well, with your vast medical training, we could just make you the chief of brain surgery. Can you fax me your résumé?"

"I want to be a tech."

Sound of crickets.

"Hello?"

"You don't want to be a tech, trust me."

"You need me. The ER needs me."

"No, you don't get it. Techs aren't normal humans. Their pay sucks, but they have to understand computer programs, deal with patients, and clean up really nasty stuff. It's the worst of all worlds."

"What's the big deal?" I asked.

"Look . . . when the bus brings in some dude with half his head blown off, and he pukes and craps and pisses all over the room, and then he dies . . . who do you think cleans that up? Me? The nurses?"

"I'm guessing the techs."

"Damn right it's the techs."

"I can handle it."

"Even if you could," my friend replied, "why would you want to?"

"Time to do something different," I said.

"Okay, here's my offer. First do this: lure a stray dog into your garage, jam a stick of dynamite up his butt, set it off, then clean the garage. If you still want a job as a tech, I'll make it happen."

"Can I do two cats instead of a dog?" I asked.

Welcome to Our Wacky World

Given that working for a pizza joint includes undergoing an orientation and general training session, it wasn't surprising that one would be required to do the same before walking into the emergency department of one of the biggest and oldest hospitals in South Carolina. The session began at 9:00 a.m., which involved me rising at 7:00 and getting on the road by 8:00. In the event you have to attend a hospital orientation sometime, here is a list of things you should *not* do the night before:

1)   Get drunk.

The reason you should listen to me on this is that I now know the material you will cover is dry, and it involves a great deal of focused listening.

The first thing our group did in orientation was watch a video on HIPAA privacy laws. Like all training videos, this one was absolutely kick-ass and was designed to be understood by the lowest common denominator, which I believe must be a venus flytrap. The best parts of the video, of course, were the examples of how one might violate a patient's privacy. For instance:

- Cut to a man standing at the prescription counter with a roomful of people behind him waiting their turn. Despite the fact that the patient is one foot away, the pharmacist bellows to him, "All right, Mr. Yarbrough! Your AZT prescription is ready! Have a nice day!"

- Cut to a nurse on the phone, with several people milling around her station looking like they are in the mood for some insightful eavesdropping. The nurse says into the phone, "Okay! Let's see! I've got your chart here! Mike . . . Adams! Okay, Mr. Adams, you say there's a burning sensation when you urinate?!! And there seems to be other discharge?!! How long has this been going on, Mr. Adams?!!"

- Cut to an answering machine. The message being left is, "Mrs. Gus Smythe! This is Melinda from St. Elsewhere General Hospital! Your pregnancy test came back positive, so we have you scheduled for your first prenatal exam next week! Please call us!" Camera pans left to husband's contorted face listening to the machine.

- Cut to woman walking down the hospital hall. She hears on the overhead pager, "Mrs. Margaret O'Hanley, the doctor is ready to see you in the Infectious Disease Department. Mrs. Margaret O'Hanley to Infectious Diseases."

- Cut to a billboard located on an interstate. The billboard message reads, "Mr. Mark Russell! Our ER staff resuscitated the gerbil after you left! Please come get him! He needs a bath!" Okay, I'm making this one up, but you get the drift.

It is, by *any* standards, very difficult to adhere to all of the HIPAA laws concerning privacy. In fact, no one is up to the task. They have you shredding paper, tilting your computer screen away from others, speaking in vague references, blacking out sign-in sheets, covering patient charts, refusing questions asked by the patient's family, and asking yourself, "Do I need to know this in order to do my job?" Please — if one of my former advertising clients comes in for a herpes test and flunks, do you really think that data is shredder bound? Helen Keller herself would be an information sieve in the eyes of HIPAA.

After explaining in detail that we couldn't have any fun by gossiping about the friends we saw in the hospital, the class moved on to overhead codes. Overhead codes, in case you're wondering, are those voices that you hear in the hall that say things like, "Doctor Thomas, Code White, east wing, 234."

Ever wonder what those codes mean? Me neither. But they do mean something. And they are actually a well-thought-out way to maintain order. For instance, instead of using the PA to scream, "*Sweet Mother Mary, half the freakin' hospital is on fire! Run like hell!*" a bored voice will calmly announce "Code Red, west wing, second floor." That way, if you are laid up in a body cast on the second floor of the west wing, you will think, "Mmmm, Code Red on my floor. Must mean cherry Jell-O!" The thought of the impending cherry Jell-O will keep you calm while the plaster encasing your body melts to your skin.

Let's see . . . The coding system also offers a better way to say, "*Listen up, people! There was a train derailment, and we've got about two hundred fifty victims on the way in various states of dead!*" Instead, they just announce, "Code Triage." You'd be amazed at all the coding going on that just bypasses you and me. There's Code Yellow for "an individual out of control," and Code Adam for "a child abduction," and Code Orange for "a bomb threat." I don't know if they have a code for TV-lawyer-in-the-house, but I'm betting they do.

We also learned safety and reaction procedures, with particular emphasis on fire safety. They had two acronyms we had to learn, the first of which was for using the fire extinguisher: PASS — **Pull** the pin. **Aim** at the fire. **Squeeze** the handle. **Sweeping** motion. The next acronym was for fire reaction procedures, and that one was RACE — **Rescue** those in danger. **Activate** the fire alarm. **Contain** the fire. **Extinguish** the fire. I knew I would have no trouble remembering those acronyms, because I invented my own: PLOW — **Please Leap Outta** my **Way.** With those three memorized, my escape trifecta was complete, since it's certain I will PASS a fire extinguisher as they watch me PLOW over little kids when I RACE from the burning building.

Another area of study was the hospital's mission statement. (This, of course, gave me the shivers, having been involved in dozens of these mind-numbing exercises back in my advertising days.) The mission statement for the hospital was the usual deal, which said in essence, "We will cheerfully work around the clock with no food or pay, solely for the privilege of saving lives, because serving others is far more important to us than silly things like making payroll and staying in business." Do you ever wonder what management thinks about when they come up with these whoppers? I mean, the boys upstairs really do sweat this stuff, as if the janitor is going to read it and suddenly be willing to work off-the-clock hours to ensure his toilets *"achieve the level of excellence needed to compete and lead in today's competitive market."* Or the single-parent receptionist is going to miss Brittany's soccer game because *"fostering creative solutions demands an exceptional work ethic."* Does anyone think that a single, solitary *second* of extra work has *ever* been done because of a mission statement? Or that a single creative idea has been developed because "creativity" was mentioned as a part of the mission?

> CEO: All right, let me see the designs for this year's cars.
> ENGINEER: Here you go, big guy.
> CEO: They look like freakin' boxes with wheels.
> ENGINEER: Freakin' boxes with wheels . . . perfect name, chief!
> CEO: Dammit, our mission statement calls for *creative* solutions to engineering challenges.
> ENGINEER: What??!! I didn't realize *that* was in the mission statement. One cold-fusion flying car, coming up!

Finally, we came to a topic that I latched onto like a Hollywood actor to a stupid cause: infection prevention. For me, this was the Holy Grail of the orientation, because avoiding infection stood out as my primary goal. People in the hospital are *sick,* and if I can go to the hospital and avoid getting sick, then I can . . . well, avoid going to the hospital.

Under this topic, our instructor advised us to "treat every person as if they have an infectious disease, and treat every surface as if it has an infectious disease on it."

This is good advice . . . although it will be slightly difficult for me to perform my duties at the hospital while remaining three miles away from it.

Baptism by Fire

The first thing that struck me when I entered the ER to begin my tour of duty as a tech was the near silence that filled the air. The nurses moved up and down the halls between the sixteen examination rooms, and the doctors clicked away on their automated "patient charting" systems, and that was it. It should be, of course, more like the movies or television, where everyone is rushing around with their lab coats flapping and barking urgent demands for 10 ccs of Thorazine, stat! At the very least one expects to see a crash team in action, with Goose from *Top Gun* holding those shocker thingies and shouting, "Clear!"

There was none of that. No doctors with sweat pouring down their brow, no nurses quietly crying because of a dead patient "who'd fought so hard," no car crash victims inspiring their jaded surgeon with the proclamation, "I *will* walk again." No, it was mostly just the hum of computers, and people behind the counter trying to track down the family physicians of the patients who sat in the exam rooms.

My buddy, who'd gotten me the gig, was with a patient, so I wandered the halls and poked around the break room and storage areas. The most noticeable feature of the place was . . . Post-it notes. That's right — like my old boss at the ice cream parlor, the team in the ER used Post-it notes to convey their frustrations about proper protocol. But instead of *Wash the milkshake machine!* the ER notes said things like:

Log the patient code when you do an EKG!
Do not put ANYTHING on the Crash Cart!
Remember to RECHARGE the defibrillator!
Act like you CARE when you tell a family that Grammie is dead!

And while, yes, these reminders are perhaps more important than *Remember to cover the sugar cones!* they are no doubt equally ineffective.

When my buddy finally emerged, he told me to just follow him around to get a feel for the place. I asked him if there wasn't some work for me to do.

"Prioleau," he said, "the other doctors agreed to bring you in because they thought it was funny. The *first* shift you work here and *do* actual tech stuff, you'll run screaming out the door."

"I can handle it, mister."

"Okay. Follow me."

We walked down the hallway to Room 12, where a 435-year-old man lay on his back, stewing in the smell of diarrhea. My buddy chatted with the patient and his daughter, while I tried to forget that all smells are particulate.

"We'll shoot some X-rays and be back with you directly," my buddy said to the daughter. As we walked back down the hall towards the command center, he said to me, "We've got to get him cleaned up to shoot the X-rays. The towels and wipes are in that closet, but remember that diarrhea can be infectious. Don't get any on you."

"Just a thought, but maybe you were right, uh, you know, about me working a few shifts . . . to get *used* to things before doing, you know, actual tech stuff."

"Screaming out the door," my buddy said, as he sat down to begin charting Mr. Diarrhea. "First shift."

After several minutes of clicking on the patient info software, it was off to Room 6, where a tough-looking black man sat on a stretcher.

"What brings you here tonight?" my buddy asked. It soon became clear that all ER docs do this, even though they have already reviewed the triage notes.

"I can't take the pain in my nose anymore," he said. "The barber trimmed my nose hairs, and my nose got infected."

Just looking at the abscess emerging from this guy's nose, and the swelling that surrounded it, made my muscles involuntarily retract. My buddy had him lie back, and he probed around a bit.

"We're going to have to drain it," my buddy explained. "And I refuse to lie to my valued patients. It's going to hurt."

Those are four words you never want to hear from a man who spends twelve-hour shifts immersed in the business of pain.

My buddy numbed and cleaned the area, and said, "Unfortunately, the numbing agent fails to penetrate infection. Are you ready, my new friend?"

The guy nodded. This particular moment found me pushed so far back into the corner, I could have been mistaken for a coat rack.

"Prioleau, please come apply upward pressure to my

friend's nose so that I might have a more exact view of ground zero."

"Screaming out the door," I thought.

When the scalpel cut the cyst, it was just a tad bit less dramatic than when a sperm whale breaches and blows. A fifty-five-gallon drum of pus came exploding forth, and tears flowed from both the patient's face (due to his pain) and mine (due to my sobriety). My buddy wrenched the patient's nose around, and drained all of the horror, then pulled out this rope-looking stuff and packed it into the hole the cyst left behind.

"Done," he said. "How do you feel?"

"Like someone just knifed me in the #$&% nose!"

"Perfect," my pal replied. "Now I'm going to inject into you enough antibiotics to cure mad cow disease, but you must refrain from your desire to explore your nostrils with your digits."

"You can amputate my damn hands if it'll help me avoid that procedure again."

"Take care," my buddy said, exiting the room with me in tow.

"Quick question," I asked, trailing behind him as we headed back to the command center. "Who in the hell is the guy who inhabits your body when you see patients? You sound like one of the Three Musketeers mid-swordfight."

"That? That's my Medical Doctor mode. Patients don't want some regular schmo like me or you making medical decisions . . . They want Errol Flynn. You should try it sometime. People love it."

This first shift wore on, and yielded copious notes. The general flow of the ER really isn't that hard to understand, especially in the cases that involve a nonemergency. It goes like this:

1) Patient checks in with the nurse at the triage window, and the nurse analyzes how big of an emergency "My urine smells funny" is.

2) Patient with the funny urine eventually gets called out of the waiting area and put into an exam room, while the doctor deals with people who are actually sick.

3) When the time comes that the doctor has seen *all* the patients who are actually sick, and by some miracle there isn't another one rolling in the door, the funny-urine woman gets seen.

4) The funny-smelling urine woman makes a comment about how long she's been waiting, and the doctor apologizes for wasting so much time on the World War II vet in the next room who was having chest pain.

5) Urine Girl proudly states that she refuses to drink water, and opts for Mountain Dew as her sole liquid refreshment.

6) Doctor tells Urine Girl he'll order some tests and be back shortly.

7) Urine Girl discovers that the doctor meant "shortly" in geological time.

"Aha!" my buddy said, clickity-clacking away on Urine Girl's computerized chart. "Most excellent. You're here to witness an official drug shopper."

"What is a drug shopper?"

"A drug shopper is someone who has developed a taste for the finer things in life — Darvon, Percocet, Dilaudid, OxyContin — all those little pills that make *American Idol* bearable. Unfortunately, the good stuff can't just be bought from the dealer in the trailer next door, so they come to the ER — in the most horrifying of pain — in hopes of getting a new 'scrip. Sometimes they do, and sometimes they don't. And sometimes . . . they run into me."

"Meaning?"

"Watch, and learn."

We entered the room of the drug shopper, which my buddy explained he was able to instantly identify by the fact that her chart indicated a visit to the ER at least once every month. The shopper was lying in bed, her face turned up and away from the door, gnarled into a grimace usually reserved for people who are in the act of being eaten alive by piranha. My buddy stepped right into the ring:

DOC: Hi, I'm your doctor. What brings you to the ER?
PATIENT: Aaaaarghh. Oof. Uhhhh.
DOC: Ah, yes. Great pain. Where does it hurt?
PATIENT: Uhhhhhh. Mmmmmf. Haaaaa.
DOC: As your physician, it is my duty to relieve you of your horrid discomfort. However, it is difficult for me to carry out my calling if you speak only in grunts. Please, fight through the pain, and help me help you.

PATIENT: I'm . . . havin' . . . really bad pain in my back. Gasp . . . Can't hardly move.

DOC: Does it hurt here?

PATIENT: Aarrrrrrgggghhhh.

DOC: How about here?

PATIENT: Hhhhrrrrruuuugffff.

DOC: And here?

PATIENT: Rrrrrrggggnnn.

DOC: Wow. I fear I've never seen someone pull every single muscle in their back at the same time. Might be skeletal. Perhaps we should X-ray it as a precaution.

PATIENT: Woooof. No need . . . had it X-rayed at St. Elsewhere last week. They said it didn't show nuthin'. Just need something for the argh — pain.

DOC: What medications did St. Elsewhere give you?

PATIENT: Muscle relaxers . . . but I had an allergic reaction. Eeeeep, whoooof.

DOC: Ah, yes. The dreaded allergic reaction. I had one of those once when I ate Chinese food and asked for extra MSG. I think I know what you need.

PATIENT: Oh . . . kay, wmoof . . . my doctor says the painkiller that works best on me is one-gram tabs of Darvon.

DOC: Ahhhh. Who's your family doc?

PATIENT: Well, he's not my family doctor. He's the doctor at the clinic.

DOC: Which clinic might that be?

PATIENT: Aaaaarrghmmmmoooofff.

DOC: I'll be back directly.

I followed my buddy wordlessly back to the patient computer.

ME: What do you think?

DOC: She's outta here.

ME: What do you do?

DOC: She's a pro, so I gotta trick her.

ME: Say what?

DOC: These drug shoppers all have a favorite buzz, and hers is Darvon, so I can't possibly give her that — it's like feeding a stray puppy that wanders into your yard. So, I go into trickster mode: just click here, select NazoNarvon, and the gig is up. She'll see the "*Nar*-von" part, and relate it to *Dar*-von, and think she's scored some cool new drug. She'll be doubly excited when she sees the 'scrip says not to operate machinery and that it may cause sleepiness. What she doesn't know is that the Nazo part of the drug eliminates the buzz, and the Nar part is an anti-inflammatory. So, on the bazillion-to-one odds *against* that she actually has some back discomfort, the drug will stop the pain, and it will make her sleepy, but it won't get her high. My work here is done.

ME: Will she realize the trick?

DOC: Oh, sure. She'll have it figured out by tomorrow night. And NazoNarvon will be added to her list of drugs she's allergic to.

ME: So she'll be back?

DOC: Yup . . . just hopefully not on my shift.

From there, it was off to a Dog Maul Guy. On our way, we stopped back by Diarrhea Man. The sickening stench intercepted us fifteen feet before we got there.

"Do we have the films?" my buddy asked the nurse.

"They're ready, but I did a probe, and it turns out the

problem isn't actually diarrhea . . . He's leaking, because he's so impacted."

"Have you excavated him?"

"I'm about to."

"How do you excavate someone who's impacted?" I asked.

"You stick your finger up their butt and dig it out."

That little gem hung in the air for a moment.

"Nurse," my buddy said, "why don't you get Prioleau to help you."

With that, he turned and walked away.

The nurse looked at me and smiled. And for the first time in my life, I knew something to be a true fact. You see, I *think* the sun will rise, and *think* gravity is real, and *think* beer is a gift from God . . . but *finally* I knew something for a dead-solid *fact:* my finger was *not* going up anyone's butt to scoop out impacted feces, nor would my eyes behold the same. That nurse, God bless her, read my face . . . smiled . . . and said, "I can handle this."

I caught up with my buddy as he was doing a nerve block on the hand of the guy who'd been mauled by the dog. It was clear the dog had meant no harm, because clearly he'd simply been trying to do the guy a favor. After all, who wouldn't want their hand to look like something as inherently beautiful as dog *food*? Here's my response if I was the physician looking at his hand:

MAN: Is it bad, Doc?

ME: Let's take a look. Holy #&%ing %#$*!!! Someone get the %#@* camera! Dude, we can't fix that! I can see the white stuff and bones and shredded meat! Put a fork in your hand, dude, that thing is done! But, hey, let's at least get a photo before we put you down. Wow. Sucks to be you.

My buddy? No biggie. He got out the suture kit and somehow put that mangled thing back together. It took an hour, but when it was done, it looked like a pretty respectable Frankenstein hand.

And the guy's reaction?

"Doc, I'm in landscaping. Can I work tomorrow?"

With that, it was back to the patient charting computer.

After watching my buddy click through fifteen different pages of data and prompts, I finally asked for an explanation behind the exhaustive charting system. It looked nothing like the grease board on the TV show *ER*, and I couldn't imagine anything more tied to reality than that.

"It's part of the game," he said.

"And the game would be?"

"The way *we* stay in business is by submitting patient invoices to the government and insurance companies. Apparently, the way *they* stay in business is by denying our claims. You know, we spend twenty thousand dollars in time, tests, and drugs saving someone's life, and they deny the claim completely because you forgot to fill in the box that indicates the patient's temperature when they arrived. So our group invested in this software, which *makes* you fill in every single solitary thing they could possibly want."

"Does it work?"

"Yeah, but sort of like a radar detector."

"Meaning?"

"You know . . . The cops get radar, so you get a radar *detector* that can defeat their radar. After a while, the cops get wise and get new radar that can defeat your radar detector. So you buy a *newer* radar detector to defeat their new radar. Currently our software is filling in enough blanks to get our claims paid, but before long they'll just invent a new blank our software doesn't know about. Classic radar detector."

Our next stop was Room 1, which held a sweet old guy who was "weak and dizzy." He was younger than Diarrhea Man but still on the north side of three hundred.

"How you doin,' old-timer?" my buddy asked.

"Feelin' a little weak. Dizzy."

"Where you feel weak?"

"Everywhere."

I looked over at the woman in the room, who must have been his daughter. She held in her hands a Ziploc bag of medicine bottles, and let me assure you there were at least twelve in there. It occurred to me they must be regulars, because who else but a regular would have the fore-thought to bring all the meds?

"Has the nurse logged all his meds?" my buddy asked, without even looking back to see if the daughter had brought them.

"Yes, sir."

"Okay, allow me to describe the plan of attack: For our part, we will run countless tests. Your job will be to lie here and provide samples of various and sundry bodily fluids . . . but we'll have you dancin' out of here before too long. Deal?"

"Okay, Doc," the old guy said.

When we got back to the patient charting system, I had to interrupt the process.

"What in the hell do you even do for someone like that?" I asked. "Isn't feeling weak and dizzy a part of being three hundred and fifty years old?"

"Yes," my buddy said. "And King Kong himself would feel weak and dizzy with the cocktail of drugs that old fella is on."

"So what do you do?"

"We'll run more tests on him than the entire Canadian health system will run this year. Some stuff will be low, some stuff will be high. We'll tweak those levels, add four or five new prescriptions to the cocktail, and admit him to the hospital."

"Oh, so you do admit him?"

"Weak & Dizzies have a pesky habit of dying. It's bad form to discharge someone and have them die in the car on the way home."

After ordering (what appeared to me) every test the hospital offered except a sperm count, my buddy scanned the list of patients in rooms. He was about to make a decision when one of the nurses slid up.

"Doctor, the lady in Room 3 says she's been here two hours, and she's going to leave if someone doesn't see her."

"Wow," my buddy replied, "she'd show me, huh? What a frightening threat."

The nurse laughed.

"Okay, let's go see Room 3. Triage notes say . . . she slammed her finger in the car door, but she's not in pain . . . Have I got that about right?"

The nurse nodded.

As we walked to Room 3, my buddy explained, "This is what we call a Better Checker . . . they do something to themselves, and decide they better get it checked out. No pain. No actual problem . . . just think they better get it checked out. The funny thing is, they want to be complimented on their decision to come to the ER . . . like we sit around worrying about whether the population is being safety-conscious."

My buddy burst into the room and asked breathlessly, "I hear you have an emergency?"

"Good thing it isn't somethin' that would kill me," the woman said. "I'd be dead."

"Good thing," my buddy replied, nodding and looking concerned. "The paperwork for letting a patient die is most overwhelming."

"Well," she said proudly, "I slammed my finger in the car door. It started swelling at the tip, so I thought I better get it checked out."

"Better safe than sorry," my buddy said. "Mr. Alexander, do you concur?"

"Safety first."

"Let's see," my buddy said, taking her finger and

pressing on it. "Does that hurt? No? How about that? How about that? That? No pain? None?"

"No, but see how swollen it is?"

"I do indeed, madam . . . and that kind of swelling at the tippy-tippy end of your finger is an emergency by anyone's standards. Now, given that I can push on it from any angle and it doesn't hurt, my years of training provide me with a sneaky suspicion it isn't broken. Mr. Alexander, do you concur?"

"Four out of five physicians surveyed would agree."

"Exactly. Now what we're going to do is swaddle this with a protective splint, to ensure . . . that, uh, it's so unwieldy you won't be able to slam it in anything. In addition, it will help you avoid looking at it. You may remove the splint in three days' time."

"Do you need to see it again?"

"Fortunately, no. By coming in early to get this checked out, you've avoided the need for us to see it again. Any questions?"

"I wish you hadn't taken so long."

"Amen, young lady," said my buddy. "But when it's your job to stamp out disease, sometimes things just get uncontrollably busy. It is a mystery to all of us. Nurse! A soft splint on this dear lady, stat. You may then discharge her."

Back at the Command Center. Click, click, click, clickety, clack. The patient charting never ends.

Next stop, a woman in Room 13. She presented to the triage nurse with pain in her ribs. We entered the room, and she was seated on the exam table in her Sunday best. Her very concerned-looking husband, dressed in a three-piece suit, sat in the available chair.

"Hello, I'm your physician, Dr. Dirk Steele. I've reviewed your chart, and you have pain in your ribs."

"That's right."

"Now, do they hurt here? Here? Hmmm, let me listen to your chest. Ahhh . . . have you been sick otherwise?"

"She had bronchitis," her husband stated. "Lasted about two weeks."

"The culprit, methinks," my buddy said. "I can hear the remnants of it when you breathe, and I'm betting you did a great deal of coughing when you had this affliction."

The husband and wife looked at each other, as if they were in the presence of the great and powerful Oz.

"That kind of coughing can strain the tissue that binds the lungs to the ribs, and the result is the pain you feel. I think we can put you on some steroids and have you feeling better in no time. And if you play in a softball league, this particular medicine could send your slugging average through the roof."

The joke lay there, waiting on pallbearers.

"Okay?" my buddy asked, sensing the heavy disappointment.

"Wellllll," the husband finally said, "we went to St. Elsewhere two days ago, and they saw her, and they didn't even shoot an X-ray."

"Fools!" my buddy roared. "No X-ray? How can one be sure without an X-ray? An X-ray is the virtual bedrock of modern medicine! I'll put in an order for an X-ray, stat, and after we examine it together, only then will you be discharged."

As we walked back to the Command Center, the obvious demanded our attention: "What in the *hell* was that all about?"

My buddy laughed. "Television has ninety-five percent of America thinking an X-ray is the equivalent of that scanner Dr. McCoy used in *Star Trek*. Without an X-ray, nothing can be fixed. Those two people are so sure of that fact that they took the time and endured the torture of going to a second ER just to have one shot. They want an X-ray? The customer is always right. One X-ray comin' up."

"So you give everyone who wants one an X-ray?"

"No way. But those folks were nice people and just want some reassurance. We call them 2-Oh's, short for Second O-pinionators. On the other hand, I might walk into a room and find some surly jerk, ask him what brings him to the ER, and he says, 'I need an X-ray.' My response is always, 'Oh, you need an *X-ray*? I'm just the doctor. You need an X-ray *tech*.'"

"I think that's the most brilliant thing I've ever heard."

"See one. Do one. Teach one," my buddy said. "We'll have you doing rounds in a few days."

Making the Rounds

The ER does not have a lock on the entrance door, because it never closes. In fact, it remains at one hundred percent alert status, 24/7/365. That's kind of weird, when you think about it — even the Waffle Houses of the world run a lighter crew at 3:00 a.m. Christmas Eve. Even the NYPD runs a smaller shift on Christmas morning — and a dollars-to-doughnuts wager says there are a total of zero cops with advanced degrees working that shift. Not the ER. People get sick around the clock, every single day. Doctors, nurses, techs — they're all there, and no one answers the phone with, "Okay, mac . . . we can unclog your heart valve, but it's gonna cost ya time and a half."

During the next couple of shifts, I followed my buddy around and learned more and more about the ER. Unfortunately, one of the lessons that emerged over and over was that most emergency room visits *aren't* an emergency. One evening around 7:30, we had a woman in her thirties complaining of dizziness. This kind of complaint gets docs a little crazy, because of the liability involved.

"Ugh," my buddy said, when the next round of tests came back. "We're going to have to shoot a CT scan. This is going nowhere."

"What's the big deal? She's dizzy. Who cares? Treat and street."

"She's a tort waiting to happen. We discharge her without everything on the planet ruled out, and she dies from a head bleed, and hi-ho, hi-ho, it's off to court we go."

"Why not just shoot the CT scan immediately?"

"It's an expensive test. And seeing how she's never even going to *open* the bill from the hospital — much less pay it — I was hoping we'd see something in her blood work."

We stopped into her room, so my buddy could brief her:

DOC: Look, we've run a battery of tests, and I can't find anything. You look really healthy, so we might have to look at this as an inner ear problem, but first I'm going to order a CT scan.

WOMAN: Well, I need a note for work.

World's most pregnant pause.

DOC: You're not dizzy, are you?

World's second most pregnant pause.

WOMAN: Yeah.

DOC: When?

WOMAN: A couple days ago.

DOC: You just need a note for work.

WOMAN: No. I was dizzy.

DOC: But you're not dizzy now and haven't been for two days.

WOMAN: I thought I better get it checked out.

DOC: Madam, this is an emergency room. You came here in an ambulance . . . an ambulance a sick person may have needed. You've taken my time away from actually sick patients. This will not abide.

WOMAN: It's my right.

DOC: I'll make a deal with you . . . I'll write you a note to get you out of work for an *entire* week, and the next time you need a note you'll go to a different ER. Deal? Or no deal?

WOMAN: Okay.

DOC: The nurse will be back momentarily with your prize.

Later that evening, we were at the patient charting Command Center, when a nurse came up to brief my buddy.

"We have a lady in Room 8 who is probably in the Transport Room. I asked the daughter and granddaughter about resuscitation, and they got offended. They're just not connected to the reality of the situation."

"Thanks," my buddy said. "I'll be right down there."

"Transport Room?"

"Yeah, from *Star Trek*. It's the last room you're in before you beam up. Or down, as the case may be."

We walked into Room 8, and my brain accused my eyeballs of sending back images that had been retouched by Stephen King. If it had been a scene in a horror movie, I would have pushed back in my chair and involuntarily blurted, "Who was the sick, twisted *freak* who dreamed *that* up?"

In the room were the remnants of a human being . . . age ninety-four — part monster, part concentration camp victim. Words fail me. Her skin clung to pure bone, her face was stretched and twisted, and her eyes told of an insanity that begged for death. Her arms were drawn up and curled like the useless front legs of a carnivorous dinosaur. And her tongue searched the edges of her mouth, like a reptile drawing scent from the air. *(Side note: I can honestly tell you that if I was back in the Marines and on a patrol in some foreign war zone, and came upon a civilian who looked that, without hesitation I would have cleared the room and smoth-*

ered her . . . and slept like a rock feeling like I'd done some-thing heroic.) Quite frankly, I wanted to turn to her daughter and granddaughter and ask them if they'd lost their minds, bringing her here instead of taking her to a hospice.

My buddy? He proceeded to examine her as if this was an everyday occurrence. At one point, he shouted into her ear to stick out her tongue, which she did . . . and then refused to retract it for the rest of the exam. After a couple of minutes, the daughter and granddaughter began to good-naturedly tease her to put her tongue back in and giggled when she refused. There was nothing mean about their teasing or laughter. It was the exact same way my wife and I laugh about the slack-jawed antics of our recently acquired puppy — except, of course, this particular situation involved a human being, not a puppy.

Words escape me. All I can say is that it was a sliver of humanity I didn't know even existed.

After my buddy ordered a catheter and six or seven (hundred) tests, we finally left the room. I had to force myself into low-talker mode as I frantically asked my buddy, "How long has she got? Like, minutes? Seconds?"

"*That* lady?" he replied. "She's healthy as a damn horse compared to what some families bring in here. She's partyin' like a rock star. Wait until you see some *really* sick great-grandmother, with the family wanting us to hurry up so they can take her home."

"Why keep that woman alive?" was all I could manage to say.

"Are you familiar with the expression 'When the eagle flies'?"

"No."

"The eagle is the U.S. emblem on metered postage . . . and when the eagle flies is when the U.S. government mails you your welfare check. That's a big day, each month when the eagle flies."

"So?"

"For the eagle to fly by your house, all you have to do is breathe. The checks don't stop until the breathing does."

Five minutes later, back at the Command Center, a nurse came in with a slightly bemused expression.

"Doctor, I got that cath started . . . but you would not *belieeeeve* the stuff that came out of that woman's vagina."

The words "run screaming out the door" came to mind.

Shift Five

"This is it, amigo," my buddy said as we started my fifth shift at the ER. "You've lasted longer than anyone thought you would, but this is the last freebie. Next shift, you're the deuce . . . the lone wolf . . . the solo pilot . . . a man earnin' his pay."

"Kid's stuff," was my response. "Bring it."

After calling on a couple of 2-Oh's and a Weak & Dizzy, we returned to the Command Center, where the Big Board stated a man was in Room 1 with a presenting complaint of "assault."

My buddy called over the triage nurse to get the deal.

"He's a homeless guy," she said. "Someone punched him and broke his nose, and he fell and injured his shoulder. He also indicated there was something wrong with his penis."

My buddy got a very sour look on his face and turned to the other physician seated beside him. "Joe? We are so gonna shoot rock, paper, scissors over who has to see Room 1."

Alarmed, I spoke up. "We really ought to see Room 1."

My buddy sighed. "That's right . . . you still find this stuff interesting. Okay, Joe . . . we'll take Room 1. But in return, you have to take the Belly Pain in Room 5."

We strode down to Room 1, and my buddy entered with the usual ruffles and flourishes.

"You, sir!" he said. "I am told you have been maliciously attacked, and require my assistance. Who did this to you? When did it occur?"

"Two days ago . . . Some dude I didn't even know attacked me."

"Ah, yes. That dude is responsible for eighty percent of all assaults. Someone should do something about that dude, but no one seems to know him."

The guy seemed little baffled but mostly pleased that he had a doctor who was at least paying attention to him.

"Let's see — yes, I believe your self-diagnosis was correct. You have a broken nose, or a deviated septum, at least. Let's take a look at that shoulder."

"Yeah," the man said, "I fell and dislocated my shoulder."

"Hmmmm . . . no, no . . . it's definitely not a dislocation. It's an AC joint separation."

"I had two guys pull on it to try and get it back in, but eventually I started screamin' and they had to stop."

"Well," my buddy replied, "that would be good, if only it wasn't the worst, *most* painful thing you could do to an AC joint separation."

"Yeah," the guy said, "it was painful."

"What else? The nurse said you were having a discharge from your penis?"

"No!" the guy exclaimed. "My penis is fine."

"Come on . . . you wouldn't mention it to the nurse if everything was fine. What's the deal?"

The guy looked around the room, as if we were in a fine restaurant and he didn't want to offend his fellow diners. He leaned forward and spoke as if he was taking us into his confidence.

"It's like this, Doc. I went behind a building to take a dump two nights ago, and it turned out the spot where I squatted was a fire ant hill."

"No."

"Seriously! There were thousands of 'em!"

My buddy pulled back the hospital gown to take a look.

"Holy $&!+! You got attacked by fire ants on your johnson!"

All three of us fell apart in laughter. The patient was pleased and between breaths made us laugh even harder.

"I'm tellin' ya, Doc! It was terrible! They was everywhere! About two seconds after they commenced, I was damn naked! Hoppin' around, swattin' them bastards off! It was terrible."

When we finally got ourselves together, I did something I rarely did, which was speak in an exam room.

"Doctor? You'll need to check the records, but I believe this may be the first case of penile attack by fire ants this hospital has ever seen."

My buddy thought for a moment, then turned to the man.

"Well done, sir . . . well done. I will be issuing you various salves and creams for your nether regions, and we'll be putting that arm in a sling and giving you some exceptional pain meds. While you wait, the tech will bring you some dinner. Now, try to take better care of yourself."

"I will. Thanks, Doc."

"No, sir . . . thank you."

Clickety-clack, click, click, click.

"Okay, we have a woman in Room 7 who fell in the shower while pregnant," my buddy said. "Follow me. This will be the shortest exam you'll ever witness."

Back down the hall we journeyed.

"Greetings!" he said, blowing into the room. "We have a pregnancy injury? Are you in pain?"

"She doesn't speak English," the husband said.

"She's how pregnant?"

"Six months."

"Who is her doctor?"

"Dennis Miles."

"That's all I needed to know."

Back at the Command Center.

"Okay," my buddy said to the head nurse, "get Labor & Delivery, and tell them we have an admit. Don't care if I admit her, or if Dr. Miles admits her, but she's leaving my ER and entering in the hospital stat."

"You didn't even ask her if she was hurt," I said.

"Doesn't matter. She fell. She came to the ER. We breathed air in the same room. I am now tied to that baby through the game of *tort-you're-it* for the next three months and up until it's determined to be a one hundred percent healthy baby. Everything that's done to that woman from now until then will be with an on-the-stand cross-examination in mind."

"Medicine via plaintiff's lawyer," I said.

"Is there any other kind?"

The guy in Room 11 had chest pain. Based on conversations with my buddy, chest pain was one of the things the ER takes very, very seriously — so much so that they created a chest pain observation center just off the ER, where they put you for twenty-four hours if they suspect *anything* suspicious. After all, if you're going to vapor lock, the ER is a pretty good place to do it.

We entered the room, and found a nice guy, late forties, lying on the table and wearing his Astros baseball cap. My buddy discontinued his Three Musketeers routine and struck up a lengthy conversation with the guy, only to find he was the picture of ill health. He had a pacemaker, had had a gastric bypass operation two years previous, was on blood thinners, and had a significant history of blood clotting. He said he had a smothering feeling, like there was a huge weight on his chest, and it hurt to breathe.

My buddy examined him and found numerous bruises, with a swollen area near his jugular vein.

"What's all this?" my buddy asked, scanning the bruised areas.

"I was in Columbia three days ago and went to an ER there. They tried to take blood, and they couldn't find a vein. They stuck me everywhere, even in my damn neck. They had five different people try. Finally, I said to hell with it and checked myself out."

"You're still taking your blood thinner?"

"No — had to stop. I couldn't get the hole in my neck to stop bleeding."

My buddy looked pained.

"Okay, I'll be right back."

We retreated to the staff physician's office.

"This guy is really sick," he said.

"What's that mean?"

"I think he's gonna die."

That, my book-reading friend, is weird. This dude was maybe five or six years older than me and looked like the kind of guy you wouldn't mind having a beer with.

"Can you save him?"

"Here's the thing. He went to the ER in Columbia, and those guys stabbed him all over but couldn't find a vein. For a guy with his history, that's bad. Then he checked himself out. That's worse. Then he quit taking his blood thinners because he self-diagnosed, and that's the worst. I don't think he's having a heart issue; I think he's having a pulmonary embolism."

"Which is?"

"That's when a clot breaks free and travels to your lungs . . . and it'll kill you coffin dead."

"What are you going to do?"

"I've got to get a bunch of drugs into him all at once, and the only way that can happen is to put a line into his femoral vein. He's not gonna like that."

"Can you give him some pain meds?"

"Pain is at the bottom of the totem pole. Pain can't kill you, but pain meds can drop your blood pressure and kill you. I'll give him something soon enough, but initially he's gonna be unhappy."

"Want me to stay here?"

"No, come on. But you need to know this: I have to put this line in . . . and when it goes in, it might cause a clot to break loose. If that happens, he's gonna be in *a lot* of pain."

The next few minutes were terrible to watch — it would take Tolstoy an entire book to explain it. Long story made short, my buddy successfully hit the line into the guy's femoral vein on the first try, but a clot must've been launched, because sixty seconds into the process the guy was shaking violently and gasping from the pain. The tiny room was suddenly full, with the bed completely surrounded by nurses executing my buddy's orders.

The question bouncing around in my head while this went on was, "Could I do this myself?"

Answer . . . I don't know.

Imagine doing your job if the background music

wasn't the easy listening radio station but the sounds of a man who's being tortured. How are you supposed to concentrate on details when the person you're trying to help is saying stuff like, *"God! God! It hurts! Aaaaaaaaargh! God! Jesus! Help me! Someone help me!"* I'm thinking your average accountant is going to make a couple rounding errors if that's going on while he's trying to crunch numbers. In the ER, however, a rounding error gets people dead.

Mercifully, once all the procedures were done and the matter was in the hands of God and big pharmaceuticals, my buddy ordered a small dose of Dilaudid to relieve some of the pain. The nursing team began to wheel the patient down the hall for CT scans.

"Will he make it?" I asked.

"Hard to say. That guy is really sick. The drug I kept asking for is a clot buster, but there's no way to know if it will work fast enough."

For 99.9 percent of the world, that would be the day. We'd leave work, drive home, and pour ourselves a big drink — maybe reminisce about our heroics while we had several more big drinks. In the ER, that's just another thirty minutes off the clock. There's no celebration, or mourning, or worrying . . . There's an endless supply of people waiting to be seen, around the clock, all the year long.

In fact, it wasn't ten seconds later when one of the new nurses walked up and reported, "Doctor, there's a man in Room 3 who states he has a condom lodged in his anus. I've set the room up for the procedure."

My buddy hesitated for a moment, then thanked her and headed towards Room 3.

"A guy would just pass a condom as a normal part of a bowel movement," he said as we walked, "but she's new, and I don't want her to feel stupid for having set up the room. So, it's time for some butt spelunking."

We entered the room to find a decidedly Brooks Brothers–looking guy. Not what one would expect to see in the ER with this particular malady.

"I understand you have a prophylactic device located in your nether regions," my buddy stated with gusto. "How on earth did she get it up there?"

"Just happened," the man replied, refusing to make eye contact and failing to catch the nuances of the question. "I bet you see it all the time."

"No . . . no, as a matter of fact, this is an extraordinarily rare occurrence and will call on all of my extensive medical training. Rest assured, however, my training *is* extensive."

My buddy turned to the cart and whipped back the sterilization cloth with great aplomb. He picked up a medieval-looking device, which would best be described as a butt periscope, and waved it around like it was a live snake.

"Sir, please lie on your side, with your buttocks on this edge of the bed, then pull your legs up into the fetal position."

The words "screaming out the door" once again flooded my mind.

Mr. Brooks was, to coin a phrase, about to crap a brick. Unfortunately for him, the brick he hoped to crap would now have to do battle with a butt periscope for control over the castle gate. And stainless steel will always prevail over brick.

The procedure was — well, words again fail me. Let's just say that whatever an ER physician makes in a year was not sufficient to cover my mental trauma.

"Hmmm . . . I see . . . I see . . . I see what appears to be . . . yes . . . oops, nope, that's just your tonsils . . . Aha! There it is. Mr. Alexander, would you please hand me that telescoping grabber thingee? Thank you. Now inserting grabber thingee . . . grabbing, grabbing . . . Houston, we have contact. Prepare for extraction . . . Ta-dah!"

The sights and smells, well, I simply refuse to implant in your mind. You don't want them there and you don't deserve them there. Understand simply that I removed myself from the room, adjourned to the doctor's office, entered the bathroom, and puked.

My time in the ER ended that night.

I sat in the doctor's office, where a tech would not be allowed, and did some breathing. My conscious mind struggled to connect to my happy place, where fountains of beer poured forth over frolicking swimsuit models. It took a few minutes, but finally my mind suppressed the horror that had infected it.

I emerged, trying to look casual, and tracked down my buddy. He was wrapping up with a coke dealer who'd eaten his entire stash while the police knocked on his door, announced who they were, and generally did the "polite, concerned neighbor routine" we demand of police these days.

"Will eating that much coke kill him?" I asked as we walked down the hall.

"Kill him? You couldn't kill that guy if you shot him with a bazooka."

"How so?"

"A person's ability to survive a traumatic event is inversely proportional to his societal worth. You or I? We've have ODed before the ambulance got there. That guy? He could drink a jug of Drano and walk out of here with a prescription for Tums."

"What's next?"

"I think we'll go check out Miss Maria Vasquez. She's got a cough. How bad can that be?"

Indeed.

We arrived in Room 2 to find a cute Mexican gal of maybe twenty-one. Cute, perhaps, isn't the right word. Let's say . . . smokin' hot. She spoke no English, so a Hispanic nurse was summoned. Through the translator, we found out that her cough was nonproductive but had been going on for a week. She said it felt like she had something caught in the back of her throat.

My buddy ordered X-rays and blood work, and we adjourned to the doctor's office for a break.

"Why are you ordering all those tests?" I asked. "That looked to me like a pretty classic treat and street."

"She's an illegal, and illegals bring all sorts of weird stuff with them. For all we know, she's got some new plague that's going to wipe out half of South Carolina. The last thing you want to hear from a plaintiff's lawyer is, 'Doctor, could you please explain why everyone on the jury has at least four relatives wiped out by the plague we've named after you?' "

I nodded along, struggling to keep my mind in its happy place.

"That last one sort threw you off, didn't he?" my buddy asked.

"Yeah," I replied. "If I had a condom lost up my butt, a slow, horrifying death by infection would be preferable to telling anyone."

My buddy laughed.

"There is an entire world out there you know nothing about . . . a world that only ER people and cops see. From the middle class up to Bill Gates, we insulate ourselves from that world . . . We go to college, we live in the 'burbs, and we simply avoid life's realities. Cops and ERs, though . . . Reality is our business."

A nurse opened the door, and said the blood work and the X-rays for Miss Vasquez were ready.

We went and looked at the X-ray, which gave my buddy pause.

"Weird," he said.

"What?"

"She's got a mass here at the base of her larynx, and there's some gnarlyness in her stomach. But she's probably too young to have cancer."

My buddy looked at her blood work.

"Great, she's pregnant."

"That's a problem?"

"Yeah, it rules out a lot of treatment options. Illegals have all sorts of things wrong with them that we never see — infections, worms, weird viral stuff, blood diseases. A lot of the drugs we use will harm a baby."

Only one of the words penetrated my mind — worms.

We walked in to see Miss Vasquez, and my buddy ascertained through the translator she'd been in the States four months and knew for certain who the father was. He did a physical exam, which included the usual prodding, thumping, and probing. Then . . . then . . . then . . . then . . . then . . . he pushed on the base of her throat.

Roll the scene from Satan's nightmare:

Hot chick begins coughing.

Cough becomes a coughing fit.

Coughing fit becomes part cough, part gag . . . then segues into part cough, part gag, part puking reflex.

Hot chick leans over towards bed, and hacks, coughs, gags, pukes.

Gray golf ball emerges from her mouth and drops onto bed. Gray golf ball begins moving, then unwinding. Worms wave to hot chick, as if to thank her for the ride.

World stops.

Nurse gags.

"Get Miss Vasquez out of here, and get her admitted to the hospital. Page the internist on call," my buddy says. He turns to go.

"And get a tech in here to clean that up."

The nurse looks at me.

I look at the nurse.

We look at each other.

"Don't look at me," I said. "I don't work here."

A registered nurse named Allison won the pool. Four shifts plus six hours equaled screaming out the door.

You Want Fries with That?

Today, I attempted to launch my career in hamburgelry. The overall effort was undertaken with a certain degree of confidence, because it was now certain that there were much, much worse jobs than frying up burgers. Yes, the fruits of my labor at a burger joint might cause someone to vomit on the counter, but at least their vomit wouldn't be alive.

I went online and filled out an application for Burger World, which, by the way, is a normal job application for this kind of job. No psychological profiling, no alphabetizing . . . just "Who are you, and what address do we use for tracking you down after you lift a case of frozen fish sandwiches?" Having taken a beating in the big-box application arena, I knew better than to expect a call right away. These corporations take their time in offering you their minimum-wage handcuffs.

To my surprise, however, an email arrived a few hours later. And the email said, "Thank you for your online application. Your application process is not complete until you visit the location you applied to, in order to sign and date the application."

Come again?

If *going to the restaurant is required,* then why offer the online system? Isn't that the point of doing it online? To save the time of . . . traveling to the restaurant? Whatever. Me just a pawn in game of life. I'll tackle the thirty-minute drive to the restaurant tomorrow.

Tomorrow. Elsewhereville, SC.

As I entered the restaurant's parking lot, a mental siren went off in my head. It was a surreal feeling, not unlike the day I walked into Marine Corps Officer Candidate School. A voice boomed in concert with my pulse, screaming, "What in the name of all that's holy are you doing here? *You* don't belong here." At OCS, the voice was speaking out of primal fear for my life. In the case of Burger World, the voice was speaking out of nothing more than pride.

You don't belong here.

I'd prepared myself for that voice, because it seemed certain it would go off. It appeared in milder form when I entered the MegaMart to apply, so logic would lead one to believe it would amp up when it came time for Burger World.

Why?

Because, as pathetic as it is to admit, we lucky few in the white-collar world, we band of brothers and sisters . . . we think we're *better* than people who work at Burger World. We scoff at their bad attitudes, and their mindless jobs, and their failure to rise above the hand that was dealt them. We feel smugly confident that, in the same set of circumstances, *we* would overcome the situation and battle our way up the ladder to success. We think that people who work at Burger World kinda sorta deserve that job, because they failed to work hard enough to rewrite their destiny.

Since I was suspicious that the voice might speak up, the issue had been analyzed from every angle. And here's my conclusion: as a child, nobody wants to be a nobody. Every kid is born to be an astronaut, or a professional athlete, or a fireman, or a famous actor. No one in the history of America has ever been asked the question, "What do you want to be when you grow up?" and answered, "A french-fryer."

Never happened. Not once.

So what in the hell happens during someone's life that leads them to work at Burger World as a real-live, all-kidding-aside job?

Life happens.

Life happened to me in my early forties. No longer able to take the torture of my chosen career, I walked away. There are a zillion little things from that career that make my blood boil even to think about — the betrayals, the laziness, the crooked deals, the politics. It was a business no longer worthy of my time.

But . . . what if life had happened to me at age twelve? Or eighteen? Life had no chance to overwhelm me back then: my parents protected me from it. My parents who worked hard, and didn't do drugs, and didn't beat me, and helped with my homework, and demanded I study, and monitored my whereabouts, and bailed me out of the drunk tank, and loved me with all their hearts. Life didn't have a chance.

But let's take all that away. Let's reverse everything about my parents . . . Let's give me a single, drunken mother, who disappears before my bedtime with her boyfriends, doesn't even know if I go to school, and doesn't have the money to post bail for me, which results in thirty days in the county slammer. What then? Am I still fated to be Mr. White Collar? Does my résumé still say Auburn graduate and a former Marine officer? Lots of people overcome horrifying adversity to succeed in life, so why wouldn't I?

Because I'm just a person — not an *exceptional* person.

Exceptional people overcome adversity, and rewrite their destiny, and pull themselves up by their bootstraps. *Exceptional* people overcome poor parenting, and emotional scarring, and dirt-poor poverty. *Exceptional* people rise from the wreckage of their past to succeed. But regular people — people like me — well, we just cruise along with the hand we are dealt. We take the punches and stay on our feet, but there's no Cinderella Man inside. We do the best we can, and when life happens, it happens. Maybe *you're* an exceptional person, but most of us aren't. Most of us are just trying to get through the day, with enough money to pay the bills and buy some beer.

For me, bottom line? You take a childhood of betrayal, and raw deals, and abuse, and negativity . . . and you shove that down my throat before I'm eighteen? I'm not walking into the Burger World to *experience* it. I'm walking in because they're hiring, and it doesn't seem like it's worth the energy to look elsewhere.

*   *   *

With the voice of introspection suppressed, I entered the restaurant and beelined to the gal at the counter. After listening to me complain about the insanity of the online application process, she cheerfully led me to the manager.

"You filled out an online application?" she asked.

"Yes, ma'am. And then got an email telling me to come in to sign and date the application."

"Oh, well, I haven't checked my emails in the last couple of days, so I haven't reviewed it yet."

"Would you like me to fill one out now?"

"No," she said. "I'll get the email, review it, and give you a call."

Okay: Fill out online application; follow instructions by driving to Elsewhereville to sign and date; drive home to await call to come in to sign and date; drive back to Elsewhereville to sign and date; drive home; drive back to Elsewhereville for first day of work.

"Ooh-rah! Ooh-rah!" I bellowed.

"Are you okay?" she asked.

"Sorry — had a flashback — thought I was back in the Marines for a second there. All these efficiencies coming together, you understand."

Okay, that's a little *Million Pieces*–esque.

Fast-forward ten days:

Let me tell you about something that will set your mind to the tune of a different drummer: not getting a callback from Burger World.

Granted, my application was full of lies, but it wasn't anything big. My educational process was reduced to grad-uating from high school, then serving in the Marines, and my work experience was simply listed as being the property manager of a Christmas tree farm for the previous fifteen years.

It wasn't a total lie. A friend of mine does own a Christmas tree farm . . . and I did work for him during the previous Christmas season for fifteen *days* while "manag-ing" the process of dragging the Christmas trees through the nylon bagging. What else was I supposed to say? My previous work was as the creative director of an ad agency, but I quit to avoid going postal? From one man's perspec-tive, it seems doubtful that Burger World wants employees who are stuck in a staring contest with The Abyss.

So, no call. Was the issue being overqualified? Under-qualified? Did they read about my "farm experience" and think "toe-pickin'-banjo-music kind of guy"? Did they see an application from a middle-aged white guy and assume "ax-murderer on parole"?

No clue. But the whole thing depressed the hell out of me.

Time to consult with the wife.

"If you drive twenty minutes in any direction you'll pass five burger joints," she said. "Get aggressive. Go *find* that job, Mr. Trump."

And so my quest began.

During the next week, I visited three surrounding cities and filled out applications at every major fast-food chain — an application per restaurant in three cities. Here are a few of my application conversations, with nary a word added or deleted:

ME: Can I have an employment application?
COUNTER HELP: Uhh, hold on. They're supposed to be over here . . . Tonya?!! Where are the applications?
TONYA: We're out. All we got are ones in Spanish.
Insert the sound of crickets as we stand there, waiting for Deus Ex Machina. When divine intervention fails to occur, I am forced to insert the next comment.
ME: So, what should I do?
More crickets.
ME: Why don't I just try and fill out the Spanish application? I speak a little Spanish.
TONYA: Yeah, that would be good. Just do your best.
Now we see me turning to go sit down and fill out my Spanish-language application.
TONYA: Oh, when you fill it out, write your answers in English.

And next . . .

ME: May I have an employment application?
COUNTER HELP: *(No response. Turns and goes in the back, presumably to speak with the manager. Returns.)* She says that we're out of applications, but you should go to the Goose Creek restaurant to get one because we are hiring.
Stunned silence.
ME: That's an hour round-trip drive. You want me to drive for an hour to get a job application when *you* need employees?
COUNTER HELP: That's what she said.

And next . . .

ME: May I have an employment application?
COUNTER HELP: We're not hiring.
ME: Oh, I see. Are you the manager?
COUNTER HELP: No.
ME: But you're sure the restaurant isn't hiring?
COUNTER HELP: Uh-huh.
ME: Can I get an application anyway?
COUNTER HELP: We're out.

It reached the point where I had twelve applications out and no calls over a period of five days. At least four of the restaurants had Now Hiring signs posted. Was there some form of discrimination at work here? Or was it just assumed that, because I look like an average middle-aged Joe, I must be some sort of defective mutant? I don't know, but I took my wife's advice and went on the offense. I returned to a site where I'd applied.

ME: *(Noticing the assistant manager's nametag)* Miss Johnson?
MISS JOHNSON: Yes?
ME: I dropped off an application on Friday, and I see that since then y'all have put out a Now Hiring sign. I was wondering if you'd had a chance to review it.
MISS JOHNSON: For management?
ME: No, ma'am. A regular job.
MISS JOHNSON: For crew??!!
ME: Yes, ma'am.
MISS JOHNSON: *(Pointing to the drive-thru window)* You need to speak to her.

At the drive-thru window is the manager. She is uniformed in enough triple-ninja communications gear to make a Delta Force operative jealous, and she is multitasking in a way normally reserved for an F-16 pilot with a surface-to-air missile chasing him. I watched in awe. The assistant manager eventually spoke with her and told me to be back Thursday at 8:30 a.m.

Thursday, 8:30 a.m.

> MANAGER: Is this your application?
> ME: Yes, ma'am.
> MANAGER: You're not applying for management?
> ME: No, ma'am.
> MANAGER: Well, uh, uh . . . uh, uh . . . I'm not used to interviewing people your age. It's just kids that work for me. I don't know what to say.
> ME: Ma'am, my wife works at home. I gotta get out of the house.
> MANAGER: *(For some reason she was now sounding as relieved as a driver hearing a cop say, "Turns out the breathalyzer is acting up. You're free to go.")* Oh! Oooh . . . you just want to get out of the house! *(Smiles, smiles, smiles)* Well, that's *fine!* Just *fine!* You sure you don't want to apply for management?
> ME: Yes, ma'am. Just a regular job. Full-time, part-time, whatever you need.
> MANAGER: Well, you start on Tuesday at five p.m. That will be training. I don't know if I'll start you on the broiler or as a cashier. I'll let you know when you come in.
> ME: What should I wear?

Wait for it . . . wait for it . . . wait for it . . .
MANAGER: We'll have a uniform for you when you come in.

Oh-freakin'-yeah, baby!

In researching the fast-food industry, I came across a fact too coincidentally bizarre to believe, despite the fact that it appears on two unrelated Web sites. The fact? The "hamburger sandwich" was invented at the 1904 World's Fair in St. Louis . . . *the same place and time as the ice cream cone.* Do you understand what the ramifications of this are? This would make 1904 St. Louis ground zero for the greatest general health apocalypse America has ever seen. At one stupid fair we launched the industries that would do more aesthetic and health damage to the "Body Americana" than, than — who knows? I'm actually scared to do research on prepackaged cigarettes and beer in a can because of what the search may uncover.

Most historians agree that the galloping gourmet who started us down this fast-food track was J. Walter Anderson, who opened a White Castle in Wichita, Kansas, in 1916. From this castle his highness provided his subjects with five-cent hamburgers, freedom fries, and soft drinks. The real plague launchers, however, were Richard and Maurice McDonald, who developed the concept of "profits thru reduction and addition" in 1948: Reduce expenses, restaurant size, food quality, restroom cleanliness, employee decision-making, and the number of available menu items, and the end result will be more profits. Add supersaturated fat and grease and special sauce, and the result will be a nation of zombies declaring, "Super-size me." With these evil genius concepts in mind, the Brothers McDonald opened a hamburger stand in San Bernardino, California, and three years later they grossed $275,000. (In 2007 dollars, that's one gazillion.)

Why did they succeed?

Indeed . . . consider the timing.

In 1945, the males of America returned from World War II, during which they spent upwards of four years eating C rations — a food that required no preparation and tasted like rhino butt. Upon returning home, they found brides and began producing babies. By 1950, you had an entire nation of combat-toughened vets riding around in station wagons, which were filled with screaming baby boomers and a pregnant wife who's jonesing for a strawberry milkshake with a side of pickles. What does this man do? He reverts to his combat training and adapts to the situation. There! Up ahead! Food! Who cares what it is or how it tastes — it will get everyone in the car to shut the hell up! You can almost smell the tire rubber burning as he diverts the car into the parking lot that bears the Golden Arches.

From there, well, the rest is history. Today, fast food accounts for forty percent of all restaurant sales, with McDonald's alone serving 47 million customers a day worldwide. According to the book *Fast Food Nation*, Americans spend more on fast food than on movies, magazines, books, newspapers, videos, and music combined. That, my friend, is a lot of Happy Meals. KFC sells eleven pieces of chicken for every man, woman, and child in America . . . and since I don't eat there, that has you gnawing on more than your share of yard bird. A survey of American schoolchildren revealed an awareness of Ronald McDonald by ninety-six percent of kids, a recognition exceeded only by the fat guy who lives at the North Pole. Here in the home of the brave, we have 160,000 fast-food restaurants, serving 50 million health nuts a day, generating sales of $65 billion a year. Incredibly, the fast-food industry employs 3,500,000 folks at any given moment.

Correction. Make that 3,500,001.

Day One, 4:59 p.m.

"Hi, I'm Prioleau Alexander, and the manager told me to report to Nanette to start work at five o'clock."

"Nanette isn't in yet. I think she's at a meeting."

"Oh, okay. I'll just wait."

After a few minutes, the waiting led to wandering around the restaurant, soaking in the beauty of it all. Over by the restrooms hung the FDA-required chart concerning nutritional information, an oxymoron if there ever was one. Imagine my delight at discovering the "Triple Bypass," which included three full-size beef patties, cheese, and six strips of bacon. There are two classes of people who might need the Triple: professional athletes during intensive training, and Nicole Richie. Scanning the chart, I noted the caloric content of this heart attack on a bun was, drum roll please — 1,310.

Add in a large fries at 500, and a large tasty beverage at 290, and you are looking at meal with 2,100 calories.

What would one have to do to relieve oneself of this much fuel? According to sources on the Internet, a guy my size, six feet, 185 pounds, could burn that Triple Bypass merely by:

- Running cross-country for 2 hours and 45 minutes.

- Walking for 6 hours.

- Playing tennis for 4 hours.

- Having sex for 18 hours.

- Fighting with spouse about the wisdom of selecting the latter for 112 hours.

91 (Yes, Ninety-one) Minutes Later

"Fill this out," said the manager, who had stopped by the restaurant for an evening meeting with an auditor from Corporate. "I've got to meet with that guy for a minute, and I'll get back with you." Strangely, there was still no sign of Assistant Manager Nanette, but no one seemed to mind.

The paperwork was fairly routine, encompassing mostly Uncle Sam's right to take my money and the company's right to fire me if they didn't like the way my hair was parted. Most of it was boring, but the Burger World Security Policy certainly inspired a belly laugh. Written in beginner legalese, it stated four essential concepts:

1)   You cannot steal stuff.

2)   You cannot vandalize stuff.

3)   You cannot sneak in at night and cook yourself an order of fries.

4)   You cannot act like a barbarian.

How nice that they'd put these rules in writing. One never knows when the need to rape, pillage, and burn will kick in, and it's smart to clarify which of the three is allowed to occur on premises.

Another humorous aspect of the paperwork was the folder in which it was stored, aka the Employee's Record. What was humorous? The entire back of the folder was the Corporate Matrix for safely and effectively firing you. All the blanks and checkboxes were for documenting your infractions; the dates and times of your "counseling" and your "attitude" about said counseling; and a big fat box labeled **Reason for Termination.** That'll get you motivated, huh? *"Congratulations on graduating from boot camp, Marine. Here's your rifle . . . and your body bag."*

85 Minutes Later Than That

"Nanette never came and got you?" the manager asked.

"No, ma'am."

"Put this on," she said, handing me my shirt and visor,

as I fought the desire to cut loose with a war whoop of joy.
"Follow me."

Behind the Door

Moments later, we made our way behind the lines. Adrenaline pumped, and my senses became razor sharp . . . What
would come first? An orientation? A tour of the restaurant?
An explanation of the various jobs and details on the overall
scope they played in the execution and delivery of America's
finest burgers? All around, the team was moving as one
seamless machine: there were freedom fries popping, mayo
getting slathered, lettuce getting chopped, floors being
mopped, to-go bags getting filled . . . poetry, and nothing less.

Time for the big picture.

"Candy, train him on the cash register."

Oh! My! Gawd!

I was to be the *face* of Burger World, working on the
tip of the spear, and closing sales with our valued customers. It is the cashier who links the GrillArtists to the
sandwiches they craft. It is the cashier who puts into motion
the nuking of apple pies and the roar of the milkshake
machine. It is the cashier who personally gathers the cash
that will be deposited into the Great Overlord's vaults. It is
the cashier alone who asks the most important of all earthly
inquiries, "You want fries with that?"

A customer approached. My heart pounded. The customer ordered.

"A number 4, no mayo, extra pickles."

"Okay," Candy said. "For that order, you push Value, then Heart-Attack Sandwich, then No, then Mayo, then Pickles, then Value again, then Fries, then Value again, then Drink. Then you ask if it's for here or to go, and punch that button. Then you tell them the amount, punch in how much they give you, and hit Change. You give them their change, hand them their cup, and give them their receipt. Got it? It's easy."

Candy wandered off, while I looked at the register, stupefied.

The register peered back at me, mocking. But, hey — I had it: provided every single customer for the rest of my career ordered a number 4 with no mayo and extra pickles. The *other* 600 buttons, which represented Individual Items, Value Meals, Special Offers, Coupons, Credit Card Payments . . . well, not so much.

The next customer stepped up and ordered.

"Sir, it would be my pleasure to serve you," I said. "But since you'd probably get a meat and cheese milkshake if I tried to punch in your order, perhaps it would be wise for me to retrieve some help."

Candy was in the back, chatting with a GrillArtist.

"Candy," I said. "Let's just say you're working with a slow learner. Can you do the register for a few hundred more orders while I watch?"

"Sure," she replied cheerfully. (Note to self: use of exaggeration as a form of humor is not overly effective here.)

Over the next hour my training continued. I saw how the cash register system had been intuitive at one point in the distant past, but that was *before* they expanded the menu to include every meat-based meal short of Foie Gras Nuggets. Over the years, it had tumbled into a semi-coherent patchwork of button pressing and re-pressing, and it certainly worked, but . . . well, let's just say it's not a computer system you would want to count on to open the pod bay door.

So that you too can understand the system, let's run through a typical order:

CUSTOMER: I'd like a Triple Coronary Sandwich meal, monster size, with no ketchup, extra pickles, and light mayo. Oh, and I have a coupon for a free Clotbuster with that.

YOU: Is your last will and testament in order?

CUSTOMER: Why yes, but thank you for checking.

Here are the buttons for you to push: Value, then Dbl Coro . . . then Coro Patty (thus adding a patty to a double) . . . then No, then Ketchup . . . then Pickles (there's no button for extra) . . . then Easy, then Mayo . . . then Monster, then Fries . . . then Value, then Coke . . . then Clotbuster.

YOU: For here, or to go?

CUSTOMER: To go.

More buttons: To Go, then Coupon, then appropriate code number for a free Clotbuster, then Coupon. (This subtracts the cost of the Clotbuster automatically.)

YOU: Your total is $112.

CUSTOMER: That sounds like a lot.

YOU: I think so too.

Customer hands you $120.

More buttons: 1 . . . 2 . . . 0 . . . 00 . . . Change.

YOU: Your change is eight dollars. Here's eight dollars, and here is your receipt and order number.

CUSTOMER: You know what? I think —

YOU: — that a shotgun is the best method for a cashier to kill themselves?

When the dinner rush slowed, a little poking around uncovered some of the instructional cards near the register. One of them was entitled "Resolving Conflicts With Customers," and featured the acronym LAST. This stood for:

L . . . listen to the customer's problem.
A . . . apologize for the customer's problem.
S . . . solve the customer's problem.
T . . . thank the customer.

Example: "Yes, I understand that the Cholesterol Wads were your favorite, and I certainly apologize, but the Food and Drug Administration categorized them as a toxic substance. Many of our customers have tried the Chunka Chunka Lard Balls and love them . . . would you like them instead? Thank you for understanding."

I was excited about this apparently new Burger World policy, because for most of *my* life as a customer it seemed Burger World employees treated me with the acronym RIP THRU. Give it a look, and see if it doesn't sound like their behavior:

R . . . roll your eyes.
I . . . ignore the issue.

P . . . punch in whatever.

T . . . throw whatever in the bag.

H . . . hope they don't notice.

R . . . roll with laughter as customer leaves.

U . . . unroll your baggie of joints and get smoked up in the freezer.

The shift wound down, with me never moving more than four feet from the register. At 10:00 p.m., I wandered into the grill area and saw an unknown assistant manager sitting in the manager's closet.

"I'm supposed to clock out at ten," I said.

"Okay," was her reply.

I stood there for a couple of moments, expecting her to perhaps ask, "Who are you, why are you in my restaurant, why haven't we met, and what makes you think you are supposed to leave at ten?" With none of this forthcoming, it dawned on me that more profitable words could've been chosen — perhaps something along the lines of "I'm supposed to leave with my cash register at ten." Oh well. Live and learn.

Umm, This Isn't That Much Fun

For the next few shifts, I kept my head down and did my thing: listen to the order; ask if they want cheese; punch in the order; ask if it's for here or to go; tell them the price; respond that "Yes, that seems like a lot to me, too"; punch in the amount they gave me; give them their change and their receipt; give them their cup; repeat. The coveted "cross-training and orientation" failed to materialize.

I was able, however, to put together some of the basics, the most basic of which is this: There are five primary workstations: the cashier, moi; the broiler crew, the folks in the back who makes the sandwiches; the cleaner, who goes through an endless loop of mopping and wiping; the drive-thru gal, who is usually the most experienced person due to the fact she must take orders, fill drinks, scoop fries, bag orders, take money, and make change, all while the next car in line is shouting into the speaker; and finally the expeditor, who scoops fries, fills bags and trays, and solves problems. The expeditor is often the manager, as this position is the pulse of the operation. Unfortunately, the manager is also responsible for every function in the restaurant that requires actual thought. When one of these thousand other duties calls her away from the position, the cashier slides down to fill orders — unless the cashier is me, in which case the cashier slides down to eat freedom fries and wonder what all those hungry-looking people are doing hanging around the counter.

In terms of assigned positions, it was clear that no one wanted anyone else's job, which is a fairly good sign that Burger World has designed jobs that feel easy once they are mastered. You should, however, know this about running the drive-thru at a Burger World, where they use the *only-one-window* system: it doesn't matter what your current occupation is (with the exception of undercover DEA), if you hired on to Burger World today and tried to run the drive-thru before you'd been there a month, your head would explode.

When there were no customers, I'd poke around to look for stuff to read and made several interesting discoveries. First, the company that owned this particular Burger World was Mucho Moula, LLC, and the particular partner who showed up to collect the bags of money was apparently a jerkwad named Steve Blazer. I surmised this from the threatening signs I saw signed by Good ol' Steve.

Sign number one was on the freezer door and said, *If this door is unlocked, I will assume someone is stealing food. I will then write up every manager in the store!* ***Steve.***

Clearly, Steve had a tight rein over his Burger World McEmpire, because the door didn't even have a lock on it.

Another sign was my favorite, because it telegraphed his total command of the McKing's English. This one said, ***Don't let anyone in your drawers!*** *If you are a cashier and you have been assigned a drawer, no one is allowed access to it! Not even the manager! If anyone (including the manager) attempts to get in your drawer, call me immediately at 555.1234! Failure to do so will result in your termination!* ***Steve Blazer.***

Sadly, Steve wasn't trying to be funny.

His third piece of brilliance demonstrated his deep understanding of labor law, leadership, and motivating subordinates. This sign, located in the employee closet, said, ***There will be no more overtime paid!*** *No one in this restaurant is scheduled to work more than 40 hours a week! SC Law states that we do not have to pay for unscheduled time! The manager cannot schedule you for more than 40 hours a week, and if she attempts to do so call me directly at 555.1234! Unless you receive permission from me personally to work overtime, you will not be paid!* ***Steve Blazer, Your Boss.***

A corporate sign, sent down from the Burger World Palace in the Sky, explained the art of the upsell: *If a customer orders a sandwich, ask them if they would like a Value Meal. If they order a Value Meal, ask them if they would like to mega-size it. If they order a MegaMonsterMeal, ask them if they would like dessert.* In pencil I added, *If they order a MegaMonsterMeal **and** dessert, ask them if they would like to make a donation for fueling Steve's private jet.*

Anyway . . . as I effectively foreshadowed at the beginning of this chapter, this job wasn't adding up to be much fun. The restaurant remained fairly busy, which kept all my coworkers at their stations. I'm utterly impressed (and depressed) to report that within our team, there wasn't so much as a stoner. It was mostly a bunch of kids who laughed when they could, and worked like they actually cared about whether they got fired. In addition, the managers were very hardworking, and actually cared about Steve Blazer's money.

A few of the interesting discoveries made during my shifts at Burger World included:

- Scooping the fries into the container so that the container is full is not as easy as it looks. Most employees just give up and pile them on top to ensure you get plenty. This is why every to-go order ends up with so many bag fries.

- I always assumed the oil used to fry the freedom fries was changed only when the restaurant changed owners. Not the case. Upon achieving the look and feel of crude oil, it is indeed discarded along with the other excess grease. This has led to the development of a cottage industry known as Grease Removal. The Grease Removers will pick up the stuff, which they then sell to hog farmers, who then return it to Burger World in the form of bacon, and the circle is unbroken, by and by, Lord, by and by.

- Assuming there were no orders voided, a Burger World could run an eight-hour shift in total silence.

- When a manager communicates with an employee, at least fifty percent of their sentences end with the words "or you will be terminated."

- Every single employee at Burger World has a cell phone.

- When a burger is made incorrectly, rather than be put aside for one of the minimum-wage workers to eat or take home, it is thrown in the garbage.

- If you bet your friends that you can eat a four-patty HunkaBurger in under two minutes, you will lose. Badly.

The part of the job that got under my skin fairly quickly was the Changed Order Syndrome. Here's the deal: When a Burger World cashier asks you, "Is that for here or to go," they are about to push a button that launches the Machine into an irretrievable movement forward. Whatever you said you wanted will be instantly beamed to every member of the team, and *that* is frickin' *that*. The absolute worst words a cashier can hear after you've committed to your order by saying, "To go" are *"Oh, wait,"* or *"You know what?"* or *"Hang on a sec."*

You see, there is no Undo button — no way to recall that order that's now being beamed back to the GrillArtists. It's gone, baby. Undoing an order involves getting the manager to void the ticket and going around back to tell some very busy Artisans that "Order number 34 for a Glob O' Fat is a void . . . Order number 35 will be the correct one." The artisans will promptly forget what you said, and then there are extra, unwanted sandwiches being dropped down the heating chute to the expeditor, who will promptly bag the Glob O' Fat *(hold the good cholesterol)* instead of the Glob O' Fat *(with extra mayo)*.

Now, with that in mind, imagine me taking an order from a very drunk house painter that went like this:

ME: Okay, that's one Gut Buster. For here, or to go?
PAINTER: To go . . . .
 . . . . . with cheese.
ME: With cheese. Okay. And that's to go.
PAINTER: Yeah . . . .
 . . . with an apple pie.
ME: Okay, apple pie with that.
PAINTER: To go . . . .
 . . . . . . with a Coke.
ME: All right. A Gut Buster with cheese, apple pie, and a Coke to go. Let me go get the manager to void these three orders we just canceled.

PAINTER: You know what?

ME: That I'm gonna throw you outta here if you change the order again?

PAINTER: Oh. Okay. To go.

Orientation

When my much-anticipated orientation failed to materialize, there was no choice except to blatantly request it from the manager. She told me to come in an hour early the next day and she would set me up with the training tapes.

I arrived the next day to find no manager, and an assistant manager who knew nothing about the arrangement. She said she didn't care if I watched the tapes, but the system wouldn't work because it was a DVD and they'd lost the remote. I decided to go for it anyway.

The first training tape was on smiling, and greeting the customer.

Let me repeat that: the first tape was on smiling, and greeting the customer.

In order to demonstrate proper techniques, they utilized the Goofus and Gallant system, where they would show:

a) A grumpy employee grunting at the arriving customer, followed by an angry buzzer.

b) A well-kempt employee beaming and saying, "How are you, sir?" followed by a happy "ding!" sound.

Other smiling insights included the necessity of the drive-thru person smiling her greeting through the microphone, smiling at customers as you assist them, smiling at your coworkers, and smiling when your paycheck reveals that you gave up forty hours of your life for $200.

Training tape number two explored the importance of and proper techniques for washing your hands. I can say only this, my friend: if Burger World employees wash their hands one-half as well as they are trained to, they are still clean enough to do open-heart surgery without gloves. Among the times employees are instructed to wash their hands are after a break, after handling food, after sweeping, after mopping, after taking out the trash, after coughing, after sneezing, after touching their face, after touching their hair, after wiping a counter, after using the facilities, after returning from the facilities, and after sneaking back from smoking a joint in the parking lot.

Tape number three was on the importance of product and sandwich freshness, and you may rest easy that the policies of Burger World are impressive. There's no way to know if employees around the world adhere to the policies, but Corporate makes quite clear that the employee has the discretion to discard any ingredients he or she feels aren't top quality. From wilted lettuce to unripe tomatoes, Corporate states unequivocally to chuck them in the trash, which is fairly risky business when you consider how much produce an unhappy employee could judge to be subpar. The other area that impressed me is how short of a period of time a sandwich can sit there wrapped but uneaten — ten minutes. Ten minutes! Are you kidding me? There isn't a mom in the country who gets to eat food that fresh, even if she cooked it from scratch! If Burger World was mine, you can bet those burgers would sit a minimum of ten *days* before that meat/money went in the trash.

Tape four explored the art of making Burger World burgers. The "employee" they chose for this tape must've been McMiss Puerto Rico, so I don't remember much. The basics, however, are this:

1) Put the meat on a conveyer system, which moves it through the cooker.

2) When the meat emerges, either use it immediately or pour it and its juices into this holding system that looks like a hard plastic scoop with a handle.

3) Put the holding system into its own little formfitting warmer. Use within ten minutes or discard.

4) Assuming the meat is needed within the ten minutes, place it on the heel of the bun and commence the corporate assembly procedures. The number of swirls of catsup is predetermined — four, moving counterclockwise and inward. The number of pickles is predetermined — four. Whether the ingredients are placed onto the burger or the crown of the bun is predetermined. The system for mashing the two together is predetermined. The wrapping of the burger is predetermined. In short, there is more creativity in math than in making one of the burgers, which is why a Double Bypass tastes the same whether you're in Seattle or Dallas.

Tape five explored the company's commitment to their mission statement, which was something silly like "Good Food, Good Meat, Good God, Let's Eat." For much of this tape they used actual testimonials from real employees, who said things like, "I won't put anything on a sandwich I won't eat myself." (Thank God.)

Without a doubt, my favorite thing about the training experience was the missing DVD remote. Why? Because there were multiple-choice training questions embedded in the discs, and without a remote to scroll up and down, you could only press the Play button, indicating you were selecting answer (a).

Here's how often (a) was the correct answer: Never.

Here's how many questions I got right: None.

It may have been me, but the machine seemed like it was getting pissed with my stupidity . . . and if my shift starting hadn't interrupted the process, it probably would've emailed ol' Steve about the newbie who was flunking his training.

During my time at Burger World, a revelation about the business came to me. It pans out like this:

1)   Burger World is open from 6:00 a.m. to midnight.

2)   The business model relies on minimum-wage labor and in-store managers who are willing to bust their hump to pick up the slack when Donny calls in that his '72 Camaro won't start (all the while tolerating dickweed owners like Steve).

3) If the service and food and cleanliness aren't at least acceptable, the folks who live in the area will just drive by that Burger World and go to World O' Burgers.

Think of the difficulties these three truths pose:

1) The store is open every waking hour, so new employees (like me) have to make their mistakes on the job.

2) There is no cost-effective way to get all the employees together for motivational events or additional training, because everyone is either at work, just got off work, or is headed into work.

3) The food you serve is a commodity, and your competitor is next door.

When you combine all these factors together, run them through a business analysis matrix, spit out a spreadsheet, and hire a consultant to review the data, there can be only one logical conclusion: run for it.

And yet the people who own these joints get rich. How can this be?

I never did figure out an answer to this economic Sudoku puzzle, and before long I ran out of time. Why? Because — thanks be to God in His Heaven — before two weeks had passed, my phone rang.

Mamas, Don't Let Your Babies Grow Up to Be Cowboys

"Prioleau? It's me, James."

James is a Marine buddy, with whom I stay in frequent touch. Unlike ninety-five percent of my friends, he had a unique take on my decision to quit the business world.

"You," he said, "are a freakin' genius."

"Thanks," I said, feeling pretty ingenious at the time.

"You're stickin' it to The Man!" he'd shout every time we spoke. James was blissfully unaware of how skilled The Man was at financial retaliation, but my mouth stayed shut on the topic. I figured at least one of us could enjoy my life.

Anyway, James was abreast of my minimum-wage adventures, and he demanded every detail. This was his latest call for an update.

"How are things in the Montana militia?" I asked.

"Everything's good. Have you followed my advice yet? There's a ton of dough in valet parking, I'm tellin' ya."

"My current position revolves mostly around depression."

"What gives?"

"I'm working at Burger World."

"Burger World?"

"The same."

"Free food?"

"Nope."

"Good money?"

"Nope."

"Hot counter chicks?"

"Negative."

"Then screw that, man! I got a job for you!"

"I'm listening."

"My buddy Champ Yarbrough has put together a Dude Wagon Train down in Wyoming. He's got a bunch of tourists from back East comin' out to do the *City Slickers* thing. I talked to him yesterday, and he's had a couple of cowpokes drop out, and he's panicked that he can't replace 'em on this short notice. You are the man he needs!"

"James, the last time I was on a horse, I broke my freakin' collarbone. In three places."

"Lightning never strikes the same guy twice. Besides, I'll tell him you're a greenhorn, and he'll use you to cook or something. It'll be freakin' awesome!"

"What's the pay?"

"Based on your experience, I'd guess not much."

"You going?

"Hell no."

"Glad you're so enthusiastic about it."

"I live out here in the Big Sky. I drive through that sort of scenery on a freakin' beer run. Why would I want to sleep in the dirt?"

"Why would I?"

"Because you work at Burger World."

Insert the sound of crickets chirping.

"I'll get Champ to email you with the details and what airline he books you on."

If you're going to wear cowboy clothes, it only makes sense to do a little research on the topic. It turns out that it was just after the Civil War when the famed American Cowboy arrived on the scene — tanned, tough, and armed to the teeth, usually found in the saddle, drunk or badly hungover.

For some reason, most historians go to great lengths to pooh-pooh the cowboy myth, spending entire pages harping on their low wages, grueling work, and high mortality rate.

Well, duh.

That's what makes the cowboy such a great symbol! Is this a nation of bankers, bluebloods, and ballet? Hardly . . . This nation, since day one, has been about sweat, blood, challenges . . . and just plain sucking it up when the going gets tough! The cowboys were the real American junkyard dogs — Confederate veterans, freed slaves, Mexicans, the occasional Indian — men who had been served the proverbial crap sandwich for the meal of life and had no choice but to munch away.

Consider their psyche . . . *and* their options:

CONFEDERATE VETERAN: I got no land, no money. This sucks.

FREED SLAVE: Big deal, dude. Before I was freed, my family was sold off to another master.

MEXICAN: Oh, boo-hoo. My entire country was stolen.

INDIAN: You want bad? My country was stolen, my entire family was slaughtered, my language doesn't even have a word for money, and now they're after me.

CONFEDERATE/FREED SLAVE/MEXICAN: We feel your pain.

INDIAN: Thanks for the lip-biting routine. But what do we do now?

CONFEDERATE VETERAN: Well, I guess I'm gonna have to sign up for unemployment.

MEXICAN: I think I'll hold a march in front of the White House.

FREED SLAVE: I'm gonna move back in with my parents and go to law school.

INDIAN: Like your thinking! I think I'll hop a tornado to the Land of Oz!

RANCHER: Hey! You fellas want a crappy job that'll keep ya from starving?

And thus the American Cowboy was born.

The primary purpose for the cowboys was to push Texas longhorn cattle from the pasturelands of Texas to the railroad junctions in Colorado, Missouri, Kansas, and Wyoming. After a successful drive (which meant, for a cowboy, that you weren't dead), the cowboys would party down in towns like Tombstone, Dodge City, and Deadwood — just the *names* alone conjure up visions of Spring Break and frozen umbrella drinks, no? For the most part, the cowboys behaved post-cattle-drive like you would expect men with a wad of payday cash to behave: they invested in booze, hookers, and poker, then blew the rest foolishly.

It was also during this post–Civil War Cowboy Heyday that we saw all the cool good guys and bad buys arrive. It was a lineup that even World Wrestling Entertainment couldn't top: On the side of mayhem were Jesse and Frank James, Cole Younger and his brothers, Billy the Kid, Butch Cassidy, the Sundance Kid, and the list goes on. On the side of law and order were Wild Bill Hickok, Pat Garrett, Wyatt Earp and his brothers, Doc Holliday, Jeremiah "Liver-eatin'" Johnson, Buffalo Bill, Judge Roy Bean, and that list goes on, too!

I ask you: does it get any better than this? Guns, leather saddles, horses, whiskey, cigars, hookers, poker games, blood, sweat, and, well, more sweat — dressed in a full-length duster with a low-slung holster tied to the leg? Men with skin of black, white, red, and tan, all busting their onions to "do what a man's gotta do"? Is this America or what?

Sadly, the era of the cowboy lasted only from about 1865 to 1890. First some spoilsport figured out that the longhorns could live quite fine, thank you, up near the rail junctions year-round, thus eliminating the need for the long, *Lonesome Dove*–esque cattle drive. Then spoilsport number 2 invented barbed wire, which allowed ranchers to fence in their cattle over vast areas, thus largely eliminating the need for men to cowsit the herd.

And that was that.

An invention was needed, some brilliant American rose to the occasion, and labor costs were slashed. The American

Cowboy rode off into the sunset, but left us with a symbol that survives — globally — to this day.

And now I was to join the cowboy ranks.

Two weeks later, I was in the airport at Jackson Hole, Wyoming, dressed in beat-up cowboy boots, faded jeans, a leather vest, a Serratelli eight-gallon hat, and a belt buckle big enough to have the Constitution engraved on it. Mister, I looked the part . . . of a complete buffoon. No one, and that means no one, had so much as a bandana in their pocket. To top it off, as I waited for my ride out front, a really cute local gal smiled and said, "You're not from around here, are you?"

Eventually, my ride showed up. He was in his late twenties, wearing flip-flops, a ball cap from Graceland, and a T-shirt that said, "REPUBLICANS: Paying for the rest of you since 1919." As you can probably tell by now, embarrassment doesn't easily engulf me, but right then I really, really wished more thought had been given to my traveling clothes.

"You Lowe?" he asked.

"That's me."

"I'm guessin' they call you the Kid."

"I feel stupid enough already," I replied.

"Aww, I was just joshin'. I'm Jimmy. I'm workin' for Mr. Yarbrough on this dude string, and I guess you are now, too."

The idea of being considered a dude horrified me. Note to self: avoid doing anything dudeish.

"Any idea what my job is?"

"Well, Mr. Yarbrough wanted someone to work the chuck wagon, but James told him it would be idiotic to put you there; said you were the best rider he'd ever seen, and that you used to train cutting horses. So he hired another guy to wash pots, and he has you in charge of a wagonload of Mormons coming from Wisconsin."

Sidebar: In Cormac McCarthy's novel All the Pretty Horses, *one of the characters, Rawlins, says, "Ever dumb thing I ever done in my life there was a decision I made before that got me into it. It was never the dumb thing. It was always some choice I'd made before it."*

"All right," I said, ignoring Rawlins's voice as it boomed in my head, "I reckon a bunch of Mormons can't be that much trouble."

"Let's get your gear," Jimmy said. "It's about four hours to Ten Sleep, and I'd like to make it before sunset."

For the tourists coming on the wagon train, I am confident that pulling into the staging area in the middle of the Bighorn Mountain Range was a thrill. The scenery was like something out of an epic film. There were horses everywhere, covered wagons and buggies strewn about, and a number of bowlegged cowboys walking through sagebrush — it had the whole John Wayne thing going on. It really *was* a cool scene, provided you weren't me, being struck by the realization that I was in charge of part of it, despite the fact I didn't know how to put a halter on a goat.

It's hard to describe my inward panic at this point. I

know *Nothing,* with a capital N, about horses, wagons, team rigging, or even basic tack. My knowledge about Western stuff is limited to one nugget: how to operate a .44 caliber Colt Peacemaker, which I was strictly forbidden to bring. As a result, all the coolness going on in and around the staging area melded together as a piping-hot cup of personal horror. Worst of all, because of my airport comment, there was no way to back out without looking like a wimp. An idiot, a buffoon, a fool — no problem. But my pride simply will not allow me to look like a wimp — even if it means getting my gonads stomped by a Samoan nicknamed Ogre. (Another story, another time.)

Jimmy dropped me off in "my" staging area, and pointed out two young men asleep under one of the wagons. "The blond one, that's Jake," he said. "He ain't never gonna go to MIT, but he knows horses and wagons. Been doin' these wagon trains since he was ten. Hell of a worker. And next to him, the one with the dark hair, that's John. John's a good man, but he'd argue with a bag of hammers. Jake will handle the wagon, John will handle the horses, and you — you keep anyone from getting killed."

Holy smoke signals, Tonto! He just described something I knew how to do. In fact, he described something I was freakin' expert at . . . something your federal tax dollars trained me for. What am I talking about? *Acting,* of course. As a Marine lieutenant, my entire life revolved around the question, "How do I at least act like I'm in charge?" Believe me, if there's one thing a Marine lieutenant knows how to do, it's *act* like they have a clue. The

Leadership Acting Method takes at least two years to perfect, but the basics follow the acronym 3HL4S (pronounced Three-H-el-four-S):

3H . . . Hands. Hips. Head. Put your *hands* on your *hips,* and cock your *head.*

L . . . Look alternately pissed and bemused.

S . . . Squint. Even at night.

S . . . Sigh. Every time someone asks you a question.

S . . . Sarcasm. There can never be too much.

S . . . Smoke, or spit snuff. It gives you something to do while you are thinking up your next sarcastic zinger.

"Thanks," I said, grabbing my duffle bag out of the truck. "Any last-minute advice?"

"We leave in the morning, so you'll want to get the horses watered, check their shoes, probably ought to hook up the team and make sure the rig is good to go — you know the drill. Just do the usual stuff."

Jimmy rode off in the truck towards the chuck wagon area.

"Men?" I said, nudging Jake's boot with mine. "Get up. We gotta talk."

The boys stretched and looked bewildered.

"Who are you?" Jake asked.

"The guy who decides if you stay on this wagon train or get sent home with the little Red Riding Hoods who get diaper rash."

"Dang, dude," John spoke up. "He just asked —"

"I heard what he asked," I replied, knowing this was the critical moment to lay claim to the role of Alpha Male. "He wants to know if I've got the brass to be ordering you up from a nap. Well, I do. Call me Boss Hog."

"Okay, Boss Hog," Jake said, as the two crawled out from under the wagon and put on their cowboy hats. I sized them up — handsome kids, hardened by a life around horses, who dressed the part for practicality, not because it made them look cool. Oh, and there was good news: now that the airport was hundreds of miles away, my Clint Eastwood outfit no longer looked goofy, and it won me some points as they sized me up.

"Jake," I said, "I hear you can handle a wagon without gettin' yourself killed."

"I reckon."

"And John, I hear you might know somethin' about horses — maybe even enough to make sure we don't send any of these big-money Mormons on to meet Brigham Young before their time."

"Yes, sir."

"Are either of you friends with Mr. Yarbrough?" (Please God let the answer be no.)

"Uh, no, sir," John said. "I don't think he even really knows either of us. He puts together these wagon trains."

"Well, he does know both of you. And for some fool

reason he thinks you two might be runnin' your own wagon section next year."

"Dang, boss," Jake said. "I didn't know Mr. Yarbrough knew either of us."

"Well, you know now. And the reason I was hired to come on this train was to watch you two and report back to him on what a couple of screw-ups you are."

Both boys' eyes lit up. Now I felt awful. Brilliant, of course, but with some awful thrown in.

"I think we can do the job, boss."

"Really? You can do the job? Well, what aspect of the *job* do you think needs *doing*, as opposed to, say, napping," I asked, silver-tongued bastard that I am. "*Right now*, before the guests arrive?"

Jake spoke up quickly. "Horses need waterin', rigging needs to be checked, electric fence needs double-checkin', probably ought to check all the horses' shoes, and the wagon needs to be organized to make room for the guests' gear."

Fortunately, Jimmy had mentioned one additional item, so I got to trick them into thinking I had a clue.

"What else? If perhaps we wanted to keep one of our guests from bein' paralyzed from the neck down?"

The boys were stumped.

"We need to hook up the team . . . Why would that be?" I added, completely clueless myself.

Jake shook his head. "Dang. To make sure we ain't got kickers assigned to us. Sorry, boss. Won't happen again."

"Let's hope not, men. I ain't bein' paid enough to babysit you. You do your jobs, I'll do mine, and before this trip is over we'll be snugglin' together around the campfire, givin' each other butterfly kisses. Is all this clear?"

"Clear," they both replied.

With that, I swaggered up to the chuck wagon, in hopes of finding the famed Mr. Yarbrough. After failing to find him, I found Mr. Beer, huddled with several dozen of his colleagues in a large cooler of ice. We had a productive meeting.

Guest Arrival

If you're like me, you know very little about the Mormons.

Sure, you know they live in Salt Lake City, and you know they have the world's only all-white basketball team at Brigham Young, and you *might* know their real name is something like Saints of Today on the Ladder of Jesus Christ — but other than that, not much.

Their story, however, is pretty cool, and seeing how it involves the Wild West and we're talking about said Wild West, this seems like a good time to take a breather and go over America's only homegrown religion. Before I get started and you pass judgment on them as loony, let me remind you of this: even though their religion may seem weird, Christians (like me) believe that the secrets of the universe are contained in some parables told by a Jewish carpenter who was put to death for disturbing the peace over two thousand years ago.

With that said, here it is:

This dude named Joseph Smith wrote a book called

The Book of Mormon. Smith obtained the knowledge necessary to write this book after an angel named Moroni appeared before him and said, "Behold! Go dig in the ground over by that tree and you'll find gold tablets; engraved on the gold tablets is a story written by my pop, the Angel Mormon."

Smith did as he was told and found the tablets, which outlined the story of a huge battle between the armies of good and evil that took place centuries before in North America. Moroni (the son angel) was the sole survivor, so he was in charge of finding someone to find the tablets . . . and he picked Joseph Smith.

As the finder, Smith was now charged with reestablishing the true religion of Jesus Christ, which (wink-wink) encouraged the practice of polygamy. (Ah, *now* it makes sense.)

By 1844, the church had grown to 15,000 members (men were fighting with broken bottles to sign up) and resided in a separatist community in Nauvoo, Illinois.

Being polygamists, the Mormons were violently persecuted. The reason for this is obvious: all the non-Mormon men in their neighborhoods were jealous and proclaimed, "If *I'm* stuck with one wife, *you're* gonna be stuck with one wife."

In 1844, tensions boiled over, and an angry mob killed Joseph Smith and his brother.

The number two guy in the church, Brigham Young, came to the conclusion that if they were going to continue with the multiple-wife deal, they were going to have to migrate somewhere really, really, really godforsaken . . .

somewhere so far out in the middle of nowhere that no one would ever again drop by for a visit.

Salt Lake City, Utah, was, of course, perfect.

During the next ten years, the Mormons migrated — first in covered wagons, and then, when money got tight, they put their stuff in homemade handcarts and walked — all fourteen hundred miles through terrain that could drive a vulture to suicide. When they got there, they got to work and built a thriving city. In the decades since, the Mormons have established themselves as the Cleavers of American religion, as they center their lives around hard work, family, abstinence from alcohol, nicotine, and caffeine . . . and, based on the size of most Mormon families, methinks the man of the house may also occasionally be "a little hard on the Beaver."

The extended Mormon family that arrived at the wagon train later that day was part movie cast from *Fargo*, and part movie cast from *Swiss Family Robinson*. They were as excited as schoolkids and as soon as they had unloaded their gear began to pepper me with questions, ranging from, "Which horse is mine?" to "What kind of draft horses are those?" Since the only question I could actually answer was, "Where's the beer?" and since no one in this particular group was going to ask that question, I kicked into Marine lieutenant mode: family meeting time.

"I'm going to ask all of you a favor," I said, taking them into my confidence as only a terrified man can do. "My name is Prioleau Alexander, and I'm your trail boss on this adventure, but there are two young men under me that are looking to be promoted to trail bosses themselves. Now, if it would make you feel safer, I can run our wagon section myself, but it would be great to give these boys a chance to prove themselves as decision-makers. I'll *supervise* all their decisions, but I'd like them to have a chance to show off their stuff. You say the word and I'll take over, but *(get ready for the lie to seal the deal)* this looks like a family that's up for some adventure this week."

"Well, *heck* yeah," said the father of Family A.

"Yippie-ki-yea!" said his brother, the father of Family B.

"Great, let me get Jake and John over here, and they'll fill y'all in on what to expect this week!"

As Jake began speaking, my knees almost collapsed. Avoiding all responsibility appeared like it might be an achievable goal.

The next morning, as we broke camp and began to pack the wagon with both families' gear, I made an interesting dis-covery. When I read in the email the words "bring only what you feel you must have," I thought, "Sleeping bag, toothbrush, change of underwear, and a gallon of scotch in an unbreakable container." Large Mormon families from Wisconsin think, "That stuff, minus the scotch, plus every-thing we own." We quickly reached the point where the wagon was groaning under the weight of their supplies and half of the family hadn't broken their tents down.

Jake had a suggestion:

"We should tell them they cain't bring all this crap."

I looked at John.

"Jake's right. I've been workin' this wagon train for eight years and ain't never seen anything close to this."

Here's the suggestion we went with:

"Men, I want you to know how much I appreciate your pithy insights on the matter. But there's a better solution. You two shut your *cake* holes and load that stuff into the wagon like every bag contains Joseph Smith's original gold tablets. And when you're doin' it, you need to smile so big those Mormons are gonna think you're either escapees from the Howdy Doody show, or on drugs — drugs so good they're gonna try and buy 'em off you. In the meantime, *I'll* go talk to Jimmy and ask him what the procedure is when *paid-in-full* guests bring more luggage than they should. I'll betcha a dollar, though, that weeping and wailing from the hired help will not be on his list of steps to take."

With that, it was off to find Jimmy to get some guidance.

"No sweat," he told me. "The gear-in-the-wagon deal is to just make it seem realistic. Get Jake and John to bring all the extra stuff up here. We'll load it in the horse trailer we bring along in case a horse goes lame."

Jimmy, of course, issued that order thinking that I would want to match people up with their horses, teach them how to put on their saddle, teach them how to put on the horse's bit and the bridle — you know, all the hundred and one things I had no clue about. My plan was better, chiefly because it entailed ordering Jake and John to do all of the above, while my time was split between chatting up the Mormons and 3HL4Sing.

My eyeballs also made an interesting discovery that morning, which was amusing and distracting at the same time. Here's the deal: Mormons are a fairly puritanical bunch, but there's one harsh reality the gals must deal with: it is their *primary job* to get married young, and the competition is *fierce* to land the available Mr. Right . . . especially if Mr. Right has family money or it seems he will be able to make his own. Because the courtships are usually formal (with dating done in groups), and "there's *no* way *no* one is getting *no*thing" before the wedding night, there's only one proven solution for landing that successful lad: beginning at the age of sixteen, you present yourself to the world 24/7/365 as if you are walking into a movie studio to audition for the part of Britney Spears in the motion picture *Britney: The Really* Hot *Years.* The point, of course, is to have Mr. Right so overwhelmed by hormones that he proposes on the way into the ice cream parlor on Group Date One.

Please notice that the time frame referenced is 24/7/365, a time frame that *would* include a wagon train trip through the Bighorn Mountain Range, a thousand miles from home. (One never knows where one may encounter a fellow believer.) As a result, the young ladies emerged from their tents looking a bit like Miss Wyoming meets Miss October meets Miss Manners . . . except entirely innocent, and entirely without desire, provided a young Mormon male with a wristwatch nicer than a Casio didn't walk by.

On the Trail, Day One

After less than half a day in the saddle, I made a couple of discoveries that rivaled the breathtaking scenery. They are as follows:

1) Never ride a horse while wearing boxer underwear. This ranks ahead of even "Never start a land war in Southeast Asia."

2) The parts of your body involved in riding do not, with time, get numb. They just hurt more and more.

Now, please understand, these discoveries are not offered lightly. Prior to these insights, I viewed myself as something of a potential cowboy, who'd simply been born in the wrong region of the country. During my life, I'd done my share of silly two-hour "trail rides" and scoffed that we didn't get to gallop, much less rope a few head of steer. I assumed that, given a chance at the real thing, ropin' and ridin' would come to me like a politician to cash in an envelope. Note the very past tense of "assumed."

Another discovery made over the course of the week was how many different types of horses there are, and how complex the lingo system is. I thought horses were either mares, stallions, or geldings (meaning they are former stallions). Nope. Horses can be referred to as their colors: a palomino, a dun, a paint, a gray, etc. Horses can be referred to by their bloodline: a quarterhorse, a Thoroughbred, a paso fino, etc. Or the stupid beasts can even be referred to by how they walk: a gaited horse, a walking horse, a draft horse, etc. Do you have any idea how difficult this is to absorb when you're pretending you already know it?

> ME: *(having heard someone call a horse a paint)* That's a good-lookin' paint.
> JAKE: Which one?
> ME: That, uhhhhh, gelding?
> JAKE: The quarterhorse, or the Arabian?
> ME: Uh, over yonder
> JAKE: Oh, over there. The paso fino.
> ME: Of course.
> JAKE: Yeah, that passee, he's got a nice gait. But I kinda like walkin' horses myself. You got a favorite?
> ME: Me? Oh, yeah, palominos.
> JAKE: You pick a mount based on *color*?
> ME: *(Cough)* I'm just joshin' ya'. If it's got hooves, I'll ride it. How about you? Got any dislikes?
> JAKE: I ain't gonna ride no Thoroughbred, if that's what you mean. I don't care what color it is. I don't need the aggravation.
> ME: I *like* horses with a little spirit.
> JAKE: Well, tomorrow I'll put you on John's dun — she's got spunk, I'd say.
> ME: I never ride duns.
> JAKE: But, uh . . . you're on a dun right now.
> ME: I *know* . . . What I meant was — Hey, is that Bigfoot over in that tree line?

I rode four different horses that week and as a result came to the conclusion that there are actually only two kinds of horses: mine and everyone else's. My horse has a thuddish, plodding walk; a violent, spine-crushing trot; and an awkward, jerky lope. Everyone else's horse glides like an egg on Teflon.

Anyway, the scenery we encountered on day one was even more beautiful than I'd expected or hoped for. On the occasions when we stopped long enough for me to reset my jarred eyeballs, catch my breath, drink some water, adjust my package, clean my sunglasses, steal a few glances at the Lolitas, retie my rain slicker to the saddle, and gasp for Jake and John to check on the guests, I'd settle in for the several remaining seconds to admire the beauty. About that time, the wagon train would once again lurch forward, and my personals would resume their attack on the saddle.

The "pull" for the first day was twelve miles, a distance most folks would feel is quite reasonable. When we'd covered what was surely 11.85 of those miles, I loped ahead to speak with the trail boss in charge of the wagon group in front of me.

"How far?" I asked, cool-like.

"We've gone about three miles," he replied.

"Hmmm, reckoned we'd gone a piece further." Hopefully it didn't come out as "Whaaaaa!" and "I want my mommy!"

"Name's Tom," he said.

"I'm Lowe."

"How you know Mr. Yarbrough?" he asked.

"Never met him. Got this job through a referral . . . a buddy of mine is a buddy of his. Called at the last second, and booked me a flight."

"How you like the Bighorn Mountains?"

"Nothin' like riding a fine horse through new country."

"Your ass sore yet?"

"Nah."

"You lying?"

"You bet."

"You got any idea what you're doing with all this cowboy stuff?"

"Not a clue."

We rode for a minute in silence. It was one of those really *comfortable* minutes, like when the groom realizes that the bride has split, and he's left standing in front of the congregation wondering who has to pay for all the champagne and cucumber sandwiches.

"What was you drinkin' last night?" Tom asked.

"Scotch," I said.

"I'm a drinkin' man myself," Tom replied. "But my wife wouldn't let me bring any on this trip. Inspected my bags, and dropped me off at the staging area. You got enough to share?"

"Lemme tell you somethin', Tom. You help trick my crew into thinking I have a clue, and you'll enjoy whatever size hangover suits you. Daily."

Tom pulled off his glove, and we shook hands. I may have been a lousy cowboy, but at least I'd made a deal with a real one.

That night the Mormons built a campfire and sang tunes they knew together as a family. I would have joined them, but

me and my new friend Tom were chewing the beefsteak fat.
Also, the fact that I was plowed by scotch and Vicodin cock-
tails didn't help my ability to circulate amongst the guests.

"What you do for a livin'?" Tom asked.

"Nothin'. I used to be in advertising, but dropped out.
Now I get hired onto stuff like this and try not to get killed."

"Makes sense to me."

"Whadda you do?" I responded.

"Used to have a real job. Now I'm a farrier."

"A farrier?"

"Yeah — shoe horses."

"Really? Man, that is too frickin' cool. You're a
dropout, too. What did you do before that?"

"Special Forces officer."

"No, kiddin'. I was a Marine."

"Wussy."

"Wannabe."

"So why'd you quit?" I asked.

"I just couldn't take it anymore," Tom said. "There I
was in the Middle East for months at a time, and Americans
back home couldn't do anything but bitch: bitch that the
war was too expensive; bitch that the war was illegal; bitch
that we blew up the wrong people; bitch that the war was
about *oil*. Oil! Hell, if there's a good reason to fight a war,
oil is it. I'd personally kill half the frickin' Middle East for
dollar-a-gallon oil. How in the hell are Sean Penn and
Michael Moore gonna fly around in their private jets without oil? Of course, everyone thinks it's just *fine* to deploy
the military to Bosnia, or Darfur, or Somalia, just as long as
there's nothing to actually gain from the use of force — it's

got to be one hundred percent feel-good, like some kinda Meals on Humvee Wheels. God forbid there's actually some national interest at stake."

"So you bagged it."

"Hell yeah, I bagged it," he said. "Americans have become a bunch of pansies. And there's no good reason for it! Think of it, Lowe! We Americans spring from hearty stock. We're the grandchildren of men and women who plowed a freakin' nation out of an entire continent filled with oak trees, boulders, and raging rivers. Our forefathers saddled and broke the biggest, baddest symbolic bronco in history. They walked straight up to that grizzly bear called Danger and bitch-slapped him around the meadow, then made him vacuum the den before he could leave."

I sat there, wishing Tom had a national radio talk show.

"At some point," Tom continued, "we stuck a needle in our arm and drained out all our good junkyard dawg American mutt blood. We became a nation of whining, sniveling, complaining, suing, Prozac-gobbling, label-warning, non-spanking, airbag-surrounded, water-conserving, designated-driving, emailing geeks."

"Tom," I said, "I'm thinkin' about amblin' over there and kissin' you on the lips."

"Fine. But gimme a Vike before you do," he replied. "My back is killin' me."

The Routine on the Trail

Lest you think the life of a dude-string cowboy is fun or exciting, here is a list of things that Jake and John had to do before 9:00 a.m., in order that we might straggle out of camp as a group sometime before ten.

- Get up, get dressed, hopefully brush their teeth, and make the coffee.

- Force a cheerful attitude into their brains, and pretend they hadn't snuck off and drunk twenty-two beers the night before.

- Saddle fifteen horses, tie them off somewhere, and disassemble the electric fence.

- Stow the fence and all other loose gear in the wagon.

- Hook the draft horses to the wagon.

- Load half the earthly possessions of two large Mormon families into the covered wagon, then drag the other half to the emergency horse trailer.

- Break down the portable tables and lawn chairs, roll up the awning that draped over the wagon area, and collect up all the trash that may have collected in our area.

- Assist eleven Mormons in putting on their chaps.

- *Un*pack the wagon in order to find Little Kid #3's boots, and the hat that goes with Teen Girl #17's outfit.

- Hustle the entire family down to breakfast at the chuck wagon.

- Fake a big smile as they watch me stagger out of the tent at 8:45 to begin 3HL4Sing.

I didn't *just* wake up at 8:45, of course . . . the pain associated with being in the saddle had me wide awake every day by seven but required an hour and a half lying there, mentally psyching myself up to be a cowboy poser. I'd stretch, and massage my muscles, and rub my feet, and prepare myself for the difficult task of looking like the Boss Hog.

When I would finally muster the strength to dress and reappear, Jake and John were hard at work and the Mormons were on their fourth honey bun of the morning. I don't know what it is about Mormons and junk food, but it's probably true that all of us are driven to some sort of destructive behavior. With booze, nicotine, and caffeine outlawed, sugar and fat are their only available poisons.

Anyway, each morning I'd hobble around and joke with the guests, and tease their kids, and generally put up a big front that it was great to be alive in the Big Sky Country. In deep appreciation for my sharing the brown whiskey, Tom would inevitably stride into camp and bellow some impossibly frontierish question, and thus establish me as The Man.

"Hey, Lowe!" he'd shout. "You see those tracks up on the rise? You reckon those were mule deer, or white-tail?"

"Funny you should ask, Tom. At first glance I thought it was big white-tail, but I tasted some of their droppings and it was definitely mule deer."

"We got a chance of trackin' 'em?"

"Nah. I scaled that rock face over yonder and found some wolf tracks . . . a couple of rogue males. They've got those deer on the move, double time."

"Sure glad you're here," Tom would say, shaking his head and gritting his teeth to keep from laughing. "No doubt I'd have wasted half a day trying to run one of 'em down. Sure do owe you one."

After Tom would leave, I would often think about the real settlers who pushed across this country, and the nature of their brutal lives . . . I mean, three short days in the saddle, and my body feels like it's been run through a wood chipper, then eaten by the New York Giants defensive line, crapped into a Port-O-Let, sucked into a honey wagon, and dumped illegally into a roadside ditch. Would I be willing to undertake a pioneer journey for a shot at a better life? A journey of several months, which would end *not* with a hot shower and a hotel room in Cody but the need to *build a home from scratch* . . . without a Lowe's or a Home Depot scheduled to arrive for another 150 years? My thoughts slowly took form:

1) There I am, sitting in a trading post in upstate South Carolina, slugging back rotgut beer and bitching about how being a tenant farmer blows.

2) The bartender says, "Why don't you quit whining and go West?" "West?" "Sure, go West! *That's* the land of opportunity. You just show up, stake a claim as far as the eye can see, throw out some seed, and you're rich!"

3) I go home and tell my wife the plan. Wisely, she objects . . . stating that my facts are, in fact, drunken gossip.

4) The wife gets beaten with a piece of firewood.

5) We sell everything, load the six kids into a covered wagon, and limp for two months in a westward direction.

6) Upon arrival at the Rocky Mountains, we find that, oops, kids 1–3 are dead.

7) Kid #4 gets crushed by a horse as we look around Deadwood for a guide to lead us into the Montana territory.

8) Kid #5 drowns crossing the Snake River.

9) We get to available land, and stake a claim "as far as the eye can see." It is very fortunate it is "the eye," singular, because my left eye, left cheek, and left ear were eaten in a grizzly attack the day before.

10) We sell kid #6 into slavery to some friendly Indians for a saw, a shovel, and a hoe.

11) The saw goes dull, the shovel breaks, and the hoe refuses my advances and runs off like I'm some kind of bad guy.

12) I walk back to the makeshift shelter to tell my wife, and find she has smallpox, and a tomahawk in her head.

13) It dawns on me that the closest place that will let me run a tab on beer is back in upstate South Carolina.

No, friend . . . this is *not* an outrageous scenario; it's the kind of scenario that becomes crystal clear once you have eaten trail dust and racked your gonads for a few days. Only then — when modern sanitation, cleanliness, and conveniences have been removed — do you really begin to understand our forefathers. Those dudes were some rock-hard, super-bad, pain-enduring, rivet-chewing, butt-stomping maniacs. Do you think they worried about the idiotic stuff we worry about these days? Their lives were one constant car wreck, without seat belts, air bags, and TV lawyers to sue the survivors. Let's eavesdrop a bit:

> SETTLER PA: Hey, what's that sound?
>
> SETTLER MA: Sounds like a baby's rattle.
>
> SETTLER SON: It appears to be comin' from that snake's tail.
>
> SETTLER PA: A musical snake? I never heard a' such a thing.
>
> SETTLER MA: Fetch him for me, son. His tail will make a nice knickknack for the cabin.
>
> SETTLER SON: Okay, Mommy. He looks like — aaarghhh!
>
> SETTLER PA: Make a note, Ma . . . Next time we have a kid we got to teach him 'bout stayin' away from musical snakes.

Notice, please, that the aforementioned Ma and Pa Settlers did not sue the Indians for failing to post sufficient warnings about rattlers. They did not attend grief seminars. They did not get to retire from, well, settling, due to the traumatic stress they encountered. They did not have snake venom declared a disease. They did not protest that the snake had singled them out because they were settlers. They did not have a Snakebite Settler Aid concert played for them. They did not have bumper stickers with a pithy slogan made. They did not declare that the economy forced them both to "settle," and they didn't have time to supervise the child. And they sure as hell didn't stand up and defend the snake's rights.

They sucked it up and pressed on.

Which, in my own small way, I attempted to do as well.

And it was only because of this spiritual inspiration surging through my veins that I was able resist the temptation to fake injury and demand evacuation via LifeFlight.

Out of the Mouths of Babes

Every now and then, the ten-ish-aged boys would wander over to where my tent was pitched. Anytime after 6:00 p.m., of course, they would find me splayed out in my beach chair, a scotch in one hand and a book in the other. The odds were tremendous that there would also be a dip of Copenhagen snuff packed into my lip. They'd sort of poke around like little boys do, say "Hi," and wander off. I figured they were digging the whole rugged honcho act.

"Why do you put that stuff in your mouth?" one kid finally asked me.

"'Cause I'm stupid."

"That's what my dad said, too," the boy replied.

"Is that really alcohol?" another asked.

"Yup, scotch."

"Did you know alcohol is poison?" he replied. "That it kills brain cells?"

"Only the weak ones."

"It even hurts your liver and your kidneys."

"That it does."

"Then why do you do it?"

I had to think on that.

"Because these hills are still filled with blood-thirsty Indians, and it's hard to sleep thinkin' about them scalpin' me."

I drifted off that night to the soothing sounds of parents comforting their kids.

Day Five

Six forty-five in the morning. Strange sound.

It sounded like a cross between a dog pacing and a couple trying to have silent sex when the kids are asleep. After about a minute of hearing the soft grunts, the gravel crunch, and the slight exhalations, I decided to investigate. I fought my way through the pain, unzipped the tent, and poked my mug out.

There, by the wagon, was the Mormon dad who said "Heck yeah," and he was stretching and preparing to go for a run.

"I gotta get back in shape," I thought, crawling back into the sleeping bag.

When I emerged from my tent to start the day, the process of breaking camp was well ahead of schedule. Jake was at the chuck wagon drinking coffee, and I complimented him on the morning's work.

"Actually," he said, "we got it done quick because the families helped. The two dads hooked up the wagon, and the older kids saddled the horses."

"How on earth did the dads hook up the team?"

"They asked us to show them how, so we've been teachin' 'em."

"I gotta develop some motivation," I thought, pouring coffee and dreaming of home.

At lunchtime, I sat on my horse while the guests ate their box lunches. This was to accomplish two things: one, it made me look rugged and trail tough, and two, it enabled me to avoid getting down *off* the horse, thus saving me the agony of getting back *on* the horse. One of the dads finished before the others, and walked by me on his way to the garbage bag.

"Man, this would be fun to do for weeks!" he exclaimed to me as he went by.

"I've got to get off this wagon train," I thought, reining my horse to go find my scotch-drinking buddy.

Night Five

With the wagon train winding down, Tom and I took the fifth night to get hard into a fifth of scotch. Most of the evening was a fog, but I found a napkin in my tent the next morning that reminded me of one of the truly brilliant moments of conversation:

"What," I asked, "is the Elvis Doctrine? What in the hell are you talking about?"

"The Elvis Doctrine is true," Tom replied. "It says the U.S. government was taken over by a shadow government after JFK was killed, and the shadow government is in the midst of a global practical joke. There can be no other explanation for the lunacy that permeates through every presidency since. Think of the track record — LBJ: didn't run for a second term. Nixon: resigned in disgrace. Ford: hell, he never got elected to begin with, and the puppetmasters couldn't have that. Reagan: he got too popular, so they put a bullet in him to remind him who was boss . . . and just look at his second term. Bush, Sr.: one-term war hero who lost to a draft-dodging dope smoker. Clinton: he got too popular, so they had him impeached. And Dubya? Only a practical joker could explain his presidency."

It was certainly a concept worthy of deeper consideration.

"Why the Elvis Doctrine?"

"Get a pen," Tom said, "and write down the names of the countries we've fought for or against since JFK. Put 'em one to a line, stacked on top of each other."

Tom dictated:

El Salvador
Libya

Vietnam
Iraq, part 1
Somalia
Iran
Serbia
Kuwait
Iraq, part 2
Nicaragua
Grenada

"So?" I asked.

"Would you not consider that the most bizarre collection of enemies in history?"

"Yeah, but in each case there was —"

"Think about it, man. There's got to be a connection."

"National security?"

"Ah, yes — I get quaking in my boots thinking about that list of A-Team tough guys."

"Well, what is it?"

"Look at the first letter of each country's name."

E.L.V.I.S. I.S. K.I.N.G.

I sat by the fire, focusing and refocusing, trying to convince myself it was an optical illusion. Fat chance.

"Be afraid," Tom said as he poured himself a scotch. "Be very afraid."

Morning Six

It was shocking to discover, but after six straight days in the saddle, your body gets used to it. If you've never been saddle-sore, this is a useless fact. If you *have* been saddle-sore, it's news you probably don't believe. But it's true: after getting pounded for a week, it works itself out. One supposes this is how guys sentenced to prison for several years survive the experience.

On our last morning ride together, the scenery was more beautiful than ever, primarily because my eyes weren't filled with tears. I was feeling good, and telling myself no one knew how clueless I'd been.

"Have y'all had fun?" I asked the Heck-Yeah Dad.

"Heck yeah," he said. "This is the best kind of vacation there is: time together, no TV or video games, no phone calls or text messages. More Americans need to take advantage of what this nation has to offer. Heck, even if you don't have the money to do a wagon train like this, there's still stuff like it. Last year before we'd saved up for this trip, we went to the state park about fifty miles from our hometown and camped out for a week. We just played games, and did scavenger hunts, and cooked hot dogs and s'mores. It was a great family week."

"Your kids are going to be fine adults," I said, a little shocked. It was my assumption that these were well-to-do, white-collar folks, who wrote a check for the wagon train without batting an eye.

"Hope so," Heck-Yeah replied. "It's why we're on this earth."

Every day presents an opportunity to learn something new. And on that day, I learned there are still pockets of America that aren't beyond hope.

Epilogue

With the end of the wagon train, so ended my great experiment. My wife and I, despite a very simple lifestyle, decided we simply couldn't continue this backward financial slide, which would one day result in five-figure credit card debt and ongoing fights over the cost of adding onions to take-out pizza. Life broke me for the second time, because — as Hemingway said — life breaks everyone.

It's hard to experience something like life at minimum wage and come away unaffected. It gives you a little more insight into how quickly and permanently life can snowball in a direction you don't want it to. And the sad thing is that it happens so early and so ruthlessly. One day, you're the high school quarterback dating the homecoming queen, and the next you're at the twenty-year class reunion talking with the class nerd:

QUARTERBACK: And just last month, they made me assistant manager of the Lawn and Garden Section. You should see the yummy mummies who come rollin' through there,

Stork! Could be some serious action ahead, just like old
times. So what are you doing these days? Been laid yet?
NERD: I just took my company public. Nanotechnology.
QUARTERBACK: Nano-nano! Nano-nano! Now you're Stork
from Ork!
NERD: Something like that.

Here's the thing: it's all so fragile. Let's say you get lumped
with Grade C parents. Not crystal-meth-at-breakfast types,
just folks who never push you to do your best . . . never
come to your ball games, or even *ask* about your SATs. And
as a result, you relate high school graduation day not with
going to college but with the "freedom" to work forty
hours a week at the big box, which is *more* than enough
dough to pay for your share of an apartment, *and* the
monthlies on that new Camaro *including* the $2,500-a-
year insurance. To the kids in the class below you, who are
still stuck in high school for another year, you are as close to
a *god* as it gets, and you start dating that hot cheerleader
who wouldn't go out with you when you were driving that
stupid Pinto wagon.

Life is good. And because you're not a dummy, you
figure you'll "sign up" for college after you get the ride paid
off and properly outfitted with iPod accessories. For the
time being, hey — let the good times roll.

But you have no clue how close you are to the edge of
The Abyss.

Any one of a thousand things can happen, and your
fate is sealed: mouth off to your boss and get fired, get a
DUI, get in a fight at the sports bar and get arrested, get

that hot cheerleader pregnant — anything that upsets the financial tightrope you're walking, and suddenly you're missing payments on the Z28. A year later, you're into the credit cards for twenty large, and — well, suffice it to say that the chances of clawing your way back from that are grim.

And what on earth can be more depressing than a kid who has blown it before he or she has even started? Worse yet is the fact that ninety-five percent of the time it's the parents' fault. Yes, there's the occasional demon spawn, but you can pretty much mold a kid for success no matter how poverty-stricken you are; those stories are so routine, they are a cliché. Kids are born to observe, absorb, and replicate behavior. And it doesn't matter if you're raised in a shack with a dirt front yard: next-generation success *is* possible if there's a parent or two in that shack working to put food on your table and telling you every single night, "Kiddo, you're getting out of here. You're going to study, and get a scholarship to college, and you're never gonna look back." I know it can happen, because that's the story of a NROTC buddy of mine who went from a shack in Georgia into the Navy as a nuclear submarine officer.

General observations aside, what specifics did I learn? What sort of pithy insights have I garnered that take me one step closer to becoming Bono?

Philosophically, just this one thing: low-wage workers are "regular folks," just like you and me. And while they may choose to read the *National Enquirer* over the *National Review* or the *New Republic* and tune in to Jerry Springer instead of the History Channel, they still have the same wants and desires as you and me. They see the same ads, and drive past the same big homes, and stop at the same red lights alongside the guy in the Porsche.

Their jobs, however, are hopeless, dreary, dreamless affairs. They work these jobs to pay the bills for the staples in life. Forget the Porsche; they're hoping they can squeeze in enough overtime to finance a satellite TV system. And the end result? Well, more often than not, they've got a tepid attitude towards customer service, which can be a little aggravating when all you want to do is pay for your Slushie and get back on the road. So, in solidarity with the overworked and underpaid, I now do something unthinkable to many of my white-collar brethren: I make a point of saying "Thank you" and "You have a nice day" even if the service sucks. It may be those words that keep them from torching city hall at the end of their shift.

From the more pragmatic point of view, I learned a great deal. In fact, you might even think of me as the Benjamin Franklin of minimum-wage wise sayings. Here are some of them from my *(Really) Poor Richard's Almanac:*

1) To avoid having a freakin' pizza smashed into your freakin' face by an enraged Pizza Man, make sure you have the freakin' numbers of your freakin' address *on* your freakin' home.

2) If you hope to have a chance of getting into heaven, have at least a fiver ready when the Pizza Man cometh.

3) Asking for a pink-spoon sample of an ice cream flavor that has no real chance of actually being picked is done at your own peril. Sure, we haven't read about any ice cream

scoopers "going pink" in the newspaper, but remember that it wasn't *that* long ago when the idea of a mailman "going postal" was unheard of, too. This is coming.

4) If you ever have the desire to purchase a fixer-upper home, drink some form of alcohol until the feeling passes.

5) Should you ever be foolish enough to act on your desire to renovate a home, take the estimated budget and the estimated number of months the job will take, double them, then add four. This will yield a more realistic number. FYI, this formula also works for converting to metric.

6) If you are in a conversation with your contractor and you are wondering if he is lying, use this test: Grab a nail gun and pop him in the Adam's apple a couple times. If he looks surprised and manages to gasp, "Why'd you do that?" before collapsing, he might have been telling the truth. This is almost never the reaction, however. He knows why you did it, and he'll respect you: it may even result in the subs showing up on time for a week.

7) When visiting the ER, know that your attitude towards the staff plays an important role in how you are treated. Be kind and understanding of how impossibly overworked they are, and chances are good all will go well. Be a dick, and, well, just remember you're being rude to the people who are in charge of how much pain you endure.

8) Very few things you will encounter in your life qualify as an "emergency" to an ER physician. Smelly urine,

scratched flesh, the overuse of recreational narcotics, and (badly) misplaced condoms will not get the doctor's adrenaline pumping, no matter how important the situation may seem to you. If you arrive, and you are in a real emergency situation, you will know it in short order. Be sure to wear clean underwear, because they check.

9) Riding a horse while wearing boxer underwear might qualify you as an actual emergency patient at an ER.

10) Rage against the urge to answer the cashier's question "For here, or to go?" until you are *positive* you are ready to commit. If you speak, be ready to forever hold your peace.

11) The next time you collide with a tractor-trailer and the fire department is cutting you out of the car while trying to find your missing leg, look on the bright side of the situation: you're better off there than working one of the jobs I've just explored.

As for me, I've found an enjoyable niche in the business world. The niche revealed itself mostly through default, as, when I was sizing up my white-collar options, it turned out that marketing was the only real skill within my résumé. Terrified at the thought of ending up back at an advertising agency, I racked my brain to come up with a different way to utilize my skill sets. Then it occurred to me: the world is *filled* with small businesses that spend good money on advertising but don't spend enough money to interest a full-service ad agency. Hiring a full-service ad

agency is like chartering a 747: it's expensive to get that puppy fired up and taxiing down the runway, and the cost is the same whether you've got the plane packed with passengers headed to Paris or just have one poor schmo trying to shuttle to the next burg. The bottom line is that you have to pay the fuel and crew bill if you want the plane to pull back from the gate.

So, my idea? Be a little fish in a big pond. Have laptop, will travel. A small business can hire me to do all their advertising for them or to teach them how to do it for themselves. And the best part? It's an in-and-out deal . . . and since I actually know the business, the clients think yours truly is a very cool cat indeed. It's à la carte creative. Drive-thru media planning. Run-and-gun public relations. The money is good, and I work my own hours . . . but . . . but . . . but . . . there are those mountains left unclimbed. There are raging rivers still roaring my name. There are horizons still left to reach. I mean, what *about* the big-box store experience? The Quickie Lube dream? Working at Disney World? Or as a Zippy Mart cashier? And who among us doesn't want to sell cooold beeeeer (!) at a professional baseball game?

These are the ghosts that haunt me. These are my siren calls. These are my tragic flaws. I am a glass menagerie of characters, pulled by the freedom outside the walls of conformity: I am Jay Gatsby, tormented by the green light at the end of Daisy's dock; Edgar Allan Poe, with a telltale heart pounding beneath my feet; J. Alfred Prufrock, fearful to eat the peach; Captain Ahab, with the great white whale within range of my harpoon; Francis Macomber, and the lions are sprinting towards me. I have the gun, and know how to pull the trigger.

But can I? Will I?

Therein lies the rub.